# THE MODERN PRINCE

# THE
# MODERN PRINCE
## and other writings

by

ANTONIO GRAMSCI

INTERNATIONAL PUBLISHERS
NEW YORK

This selection of writings by Antonio Gramsci was made with the approval of the *Instituto Gramsci* at Rome, and was translated into English by Dr. Louis Marks, who has also contributed the biographical Introductions to Parts I and II.

Eighth Printing 1980

209

ISBN: 0-7178-0133-0

Library of Congress Catalog Card Number: 67-25646

*Printed in the United States of America*

"*From the moment when a subordinate class becomes really independent and dominant, calling into being a new type of State, the need arises concretely of building a new intellectual and moral order, i.e. a new type of society, and hence the need to elaborate the most universal concepts, the most refined and decisive ideological weapons.*"

Gramsci's Prison Notebooks

"*I am feeling a bit tired and cannot write a lot. Write to me always, and tell me about everything that interests you at school. I think you like history, just as I did when I was your age, because it is about living men. And everything that is about men, as many men as possible, all the men in the world united among themselves in societies, working and struggling and bettering themselves must please you more than any other thing.*"

Gramsci's last letter from prison to his elder son Delio written shortly before his death

# CONTENTS

## PART ONE

### GRAMSCI AS LEADER OF THE COMMUNIST MOVEMENT IN ITALY, 1919–1926

## PART TWO

### GRAMSCI IN PRISON, 1926–1937

## PART THREE

### THE MODERN PRINCE

*Part One*

*GRAMSCI AS LEADER OF THE COMMUNIST MOVEMENT IN ITALY, 1919-1926*

# INTRODUCTION

GRAMSCI was born on January 23rd, 1891, in the village of Ales in Sardinia. Soon after his birth the family moved north to Ghilarza and it was here that Antonio spent his childhood. The family was poor and while still a schoolboy he had to work to help supplement the meagre income earned by his father, a minor employee at the local Registry Office. Life in Sardinia at that time was hard and the people, who had gained nothing from the industrial development of the mainland, were still living in the backwardness and poverty of past centuries. "I began work when I was eleven", Gramsci wrote later in his life, "earning nine *lire* a month (which meant one kilo of bread a day) for ten hours work a day, including Sundays, and I spent them in shifting registers weighing more than myself; many nights I cried secretly because my whole body was in pain." But somehow he managed to devote much time to study and soon distinguished himself as a scholar at the *ginnasio* in Santu Lussurgiu and later at the *Liceo Carlo Dottori*, of Cagliari.

In 1910 Gramsci left Sardinia after winning a scholarship and went to Turin where he enrolled himself at the University in the faculty of Letters. He specialised in linguistics and philology, and achieved such distinction that his Professor, Matteo Bartoli, was broken-hearted when Gramsci finally abandoned the academic life for politics.

The stages of Gramsci's life and the development of his thought during this period are difficult to document. We know that when he left Sardinia he was already a socialist, but this attitude, according to Togliatti who was his friend at the University, sprang more from the natural revolt of a humanitarian and an intellectual against the wretched conditions of his native land than from a fully coherent understanding of the theory of socialism. His spiritual guides in his early life at the University were the idealist philosophers, De Sanctis and Benedetto Croce, especially the latter. But before the end of the World War his intellectual position had undergone a profound development.

Soon after Gramsci arrived in Turin he began to interest himself in the working-class movement which at that time was rapidly increasing in strength and militancy. By 1917 he had risen to a position of responsibility and, as a result of his leadership during the anti-war insurrection at Turin in August of that year, was elected Secretary of the Socialist Section in the city. Parallel with this practical political activity, Gramsci devoted himself to a study of the writings of Marx, Engels and Lenin, which led him to reject Crocian idealism and filled him with the conviction that Marxism was the philosophy of the new society he was working to build; or, as he put it later in one of his prison writings: "Marxism . . . contains within itself all the fundamental elements not only for constructing a whole and integral conception of the world, a total philosophy and a theory of the natural sciences, but also for bringing to life an integral practical organisation of society; in other words, for becoming a total, integral civilisation." By the end of the World War Gramsci had matured into the person whom Togliatti has called the first Italian Marxist.

The essentially new feature which Gramsci brought to the Italian socialist movement from his study of Marxism was the concept of the struggle *for power*, as distinct from the struggle to defend or improve the immediate economic conditions of the working class. Looking back beyond the period of the Second International and reformism, represented in Italy by Fillippo Turati, he saw that the fundamental element of Marx's teaching was that the working class had the historical task of destroying the capitalist state and installing itself as the new ruling class in order to build socialism and ensure human progress. Since the beginning of the century Lenin had been fighting the distortions of Marxism carried out by the leaders of the International. In Italy, Gramsci was the first to realise the paramount importance of this fight. He saw that despite local differences and peculiarities of historical development, the problems in Italy were essentially the same as those of other European countries. The war had brought capitalism to the verge of catastrophe; the ruling class of industrialists and landowners was incapable of producing the solutions to economic difficulties which the people demanded; leadership must therefore pass into the hands of the only class which had this ability—the working class. This class must broaden its view of its own tasks: it must cease merely demanding partial reforms or contenting itself with "intransigent" opposition to the state and must begin to exercise its own "hegemony" over the nation, taking into its own responsibility the solution of the crisis. The working class must, in fact, recognise its rôle as the protagonist of Italian history.

The historical organisation from which Lenin developed the theory of the proletarian dictatorship was the *soviet*. After the Soviet Revolution of 1917, which aroused immense popular enthusiasm all over Italy, Gramsci wrote: "Does there exist in Italy an instrument of the working class which can be likened to the *soviet*, and which shares its nature; something which permits us to say: the *soviet* is a universal form, not a Russian, a solely Russian, institution; that the *soviet* is the form in which, everywhere there are proletarians struggling to conquer industrial independence, the working class expresses this will to emancipate itself; that the *soviet* is the form of self-government of the working masses? Does there exist a germ, a vague, timid wish for *soviet* government in Italy?" Gramsci's answer was that the Italian equivalent of the *soviet* was the factory Internal Commission, or what we should call workshop committees. These had been set up by the employers during the war, but they rapidly changed character and in the form of the Factory Councils movement at Turin emerged as a powerful weapon of the industrial working class.

Gramsci was a leader of the Factory Councils movement and it was as an organ of this movement that he founded the newspaper *Ordine Nuovo* in May, 1919. Starting as a movement for the defence of conditions of employment, it soon assumed revolutionary significance when the workers themselves took over control and operation of the largest industrial enterprises of the city in September, 1919. The industrialists were forced to recognise the authority of the Factory Councils but the victory was short-lived. In the following spring an attempt was made to break up these Councils. In reply a political general strike was called in which broad sections of industrial and agrarian workers joined in protest for eleven days. It ended in failure but the whole struggle of these two years marked a turning point in the development of the working-class movement and, among other things, it provided Gramsci with the experiences on which he was to construct his theory of the Italian revolution.

In May, 1920, immediately following the general strike and its defeat, the Socialist Section of Turin published its Programme which was printed in *Ordine Nuovo* and was subsequently judged by Lenin to correspond fully with all the fundamental principles of the Third International. Gramsci was mainly responsible for the formulation of this programme. "The aspect of the class struggle in Italy", it declared, "is characterised at the present time by the fact that the industrial and agricultural workers are unswervingly determined, throughout the nation, to bring forward the question of the ownership of the means of production in an explicit and violent way." Great possibilities existed for revolutionary advance but the decisive steps forward could not be made merely by canalising or directing the spontaneous revolutionary fever of the post-war years. Such an attitude was widespread in the Socialist Party at that time. The situation engendered a kind of false optimism which viewed the revolution as in some sense inevitable. This attitude was as dangerous as, and possibly more so than that which rejected revolution and tried to limit the demands of the workers. One thing stood out clearly: the need for resolute leadership and an understanding of the immense problems involved in preparing the working classes organisationally, politically and culturally for the great tasks which lay ahead.

However, the very existence of revolutionary possibilities revealed a state of confusion and indecision among the Socialist leaders. While the ruling class was preparing its counterblows and priming Mussolini's blackshirts for their rôle, the Socialist leadership was content to let events take their course. The reign of Giolittism—the nearest equivalent in Italy to parliamentary democracy —was approaching its end and the vacuum created by its demise could be filled in one of two ways. "The present phase of the class struggle in Italy", continued the manifesto of *Ordine Nuovo*, "is the phase which precedes: either the conquest of political power by the revolutionary proletariat for the transition to new modes of production and distribution which will also allow a revival of productivity; or a tremendous reaction by the propertied classes and the governmental caste. No violence will be spared to subject the industrial and agricultural proletariat to servile labour: they will seek to break up inexorably the working-class's organs of political struggle (the Socialist Party) and to incorporate the organs of economic resistance (the Trade Unions and the Co-operatives) into the machinery of the bourgeois state."

The years immediately following the defeat of the Factory Councils movement were packed with the greatest activity for Gramsci. He now saw the immensity of the task facing the Socialist and Communist movements and was at the same time acutely aware of the terrible dangers which threatened the whole Italian nation if that task were not accomplished in time. It is difficult to give a clear picture of the many-sidedness of his interests and influence. He had seen in the Turinese working class the germs of a new society. The task which he set himself was to develop that germ, helping it to show itself superior in all fields to the old society. This involved giving political leadership, but not only that. *Ordine Nuovo* was much more than a purely political newspaper. Gramsci believed that the working class was capable of understanding and mastering the most fundamental problems of scientific and cultural development. Even this task might have been simple if it had been approached with the attitude of a teacher lecturing to schoolchildren. But this was not Gramsci's way. The editorial offices of *Ordine Nuovo* at Turin were a meeting place for workers of all kinds who came to discuss with Gramsci the problems of the whole movement. And Gramsci looked on this constant personal contact as essential for success. In addition to being a political leader and an editor he became a personal guide and counsellor, a man who was not only respected but loved far beyond the limits of Turin. He became a sort of legend and used to receive hundreds of letters from workers in all parts of the country. To each one he gave the most careful and minute consideration for he firmly believed that a careful study of these letters would enable the newspaper to fulfil its duties more adequately. He had set himself to learn from the workers as well as to help them.

A glimpse into Gramsci's attitude to his readers and to his own tasks is given in a reminiscence of Felice Platone, who worked with him on the editorial board of the newspaper. One day Gramsci was visited in his office by a young university lecturer who, says Platone, was one of those people "who can, without any difficulty and with a smile on his lips, through inborn genius, answer any question, pass a judgment on any event and reject any objection with supreme disdain. . . ."

Platone continues: "The imperceptible frown with which Gramsci welcomed the newcomer made me assume that if I stayed I would not be wasting my time, and I began conscientiously looking for a newspaper in the heap which cluttered up my desk, savouring the dialogue which was about to unfold. The young professor said that he intended to 'help' the workers, 'instruct them', 'educate them', and all this disinterestedly. The workers would have in him a loyal and capable 'teacher'. From the beginning Gramsci fumed in silence; he kept taking off and putting on his spectacles. I saw that he was about to lose his patience. Then he calmed down and listened to the end, without raising his eyes, entirely absorbed in folding and refolding, with great care, a sheet of paper. When the professor had finished, Gramsci, as if he had heard nothing and had been thinking about something completely different, asked him:

" 'What in your opinion was the most fruitful and important step forward made by man after he had learned to use fire?'

"When he saw that the other man gaped astonishedly, he continued:

" 'Excuse me, this really is not good enough. But tell me, how many years have you been at school with the workers?'

" 'Really, I never intended to become a worker . . .'

" 'That is not what I meant. Who do you think is more qualified to be classed as an intellectual: a lecturer, or even a professor, who has stored up a certain number of more or less disconnected notions and ideas, who knows nothing except his own job; or a worker, even a not very cultured worker, but one who has a clear idea of what the progress and future of the world should be and who coherently organises and co-ordinates those modest and elementary notions he has been able to acquire around this idea?'

" 'But I know Marxism very well; moreover, I have given it an idealistic basis.'

"That was enough for Gramsci. After a few minutes the professor, as if by magic, had lost his affectation and went away saying, in the tone of one who does not want to show his wounded pride: 'I shall think about his advice to learn from the workers.' "

But Platone adds that Gramsci devoted much of his time to the study of intellectual movements outside the working-class camp. Those who read the prison notebooks can be left in no doubt as to the enormous breadth of his reading and knowledge of contemporary developments, but it is worthwhile recording that in the period about which we are talking Gramsci was permanent dramatic critic for the Socialist organ *Avanti!* At a later date he gave one of the first appraisals of the importance of the dramatic work of Pirandello. While in prison he composed a series of acute observations on the significance of the tenth canto of Dante's *Inferno.* His interests were in fact encyclopaedic and at the same time they were united in a single organic concept of the struggle for the development of a new society, of which *Ordine Nuovo* was the first and most daring expression. In that struggle the intellectuals had a definite and important rôle to play, but only as intellectuals of the working class, accepting the fact that it was this class alone which carried within it the seeds of the new society. "What a tragedy it would be", he wrote to a comrade in 1924, "if the groups of intellectuals who come to the working class and in whom the working class places its trust, do not feel themselves the same flesh and blood as the most humble, the most backward, and the least aware of our workers and peasants. All our work would be useless and we would obtain no result."

The outcome of the new perspectives opened up by the events of 1919 and 1920 together with the work of the *Ordine Nuovo* group, was the formation in 1921 of the Italian Communist Party. The programme of May, 1920, from which we have already quoted, had continued its analysis of the situation in the following words:

"The working class and peasant forces lack co-ordination and revolutionary concentration, because the leading organs of the Socialist Party have shown that they understand absolutely nothing about the development of national and international history in the present period, and that they understand nothing of the mission incumbent on the organs of struggle of the revolutionary proletariat. The Socialist Party looks on as a spectator at the unfolding of events, it never has its own opinion to show that it is dependent on the revolutionary theses of Marxism and the Communist International, it does not issue directives of a kind which can be understood by the masses, giving a general direction, unifying and concentrating revolutionary action."

The break with the Socialist leadership and the formation of the Italian Communist Party came finally at the Livorno Congress in January, 1921, and it marks in a certain sense the last major revolutionary development of the post-war period. As the strength of Fascism and militant nationalism of the D'Annunzio type began to increase, the character of the struggle changed and rapidly began to take on the form of a fight to preserve democratic liberties by the organisation of powerfully united and effective action. Gramsci was one of the first to realise the full meaning of the change. Inside the Communist

Party he carried on an incessant campaign against all forms of sectarianism and particularly that of the first secretary of the Party, Bordiga, who believed that Fascism was simply another form of bourgeois rule and that the tactics in fighting it should remain unchanged. To this suicidal policy Gramsci opposed the policy of giving maximum support to all forms of popular resistance to Fascism, and he eventually succeeded in winning the Party for support of the idea of a united front. In 1924, after his return from Russia, where he went for health reasons, he was elected secretary of the Communist Party.

Gramsci now began a thorough reorganisation of the Party to meet the new situation and the new tasks. In the prevailing conditions of semi-illegality and constant terrorisation which followed the March on Rome, in October 1922, *Ordine Nuovo* had been forced to cease publication. In March, 1924 Gramsci founded a new newspaper, *Unità*, whose title proclaimed its aims. In the following April, elections were held for Parliament, and despite Fascist intimidation, which included the assassination of one Socialist candidate and numerous acts of terrorism, the people returned an unprecedented number of Communist and Socialist candidates. Among the Communists elected was Gramsci himself.

But Mussolini acted before the new policy could prove fully effective. At the opening of the new Parliament, Giacomo Matteotti, a Socialist deputy, denounced the corrupt and undemocratic way in which the elections had been conducted. Shortly afterwards he was assassinated in circumstances which ₚointed to the direct complicity of the government. This action opened up a grave crisis. The democratic opposition left Parliament and began a campaign denouncing this latest atrocity and calling on the king to dismiss Mussolini. Naturally, the king temporised while Mussolini played for time. Gramsci, together with the other Communist deputies, joined the Parliamentary opposition but insisted that it was impossible to act effectively inside the constitution. He proposed the declaration of a general strike against Fascism, but the proposal was rejected by the other parties, who blindly thought that their strength lay in remaining within the law and waiting for the monarchy to intervene. Even the Parliamentary Socialist Party followed this line and the Communists remained isolated.

As no decisive action was taken Mussolini felt that the immediate crisis had passed and reopened Parliament, which he had closed after the walk-out of the opposition. At this point Gramsci decided to leave the Aventine (as the opposition parties were called), lead the Communist deputies back into Parliament, and continued to denounce Fascism from there. The impotence of the democratic parties had been shown clearly and Gramsci's prompt action resulted in a considerable enhancing of the position of the Communist Party as a leader in the fight against Mussolini. Gramsci saw that this fight could not be confined to verbal protests; it must be coupled with an immense broadening of the whole political and economic struggle of the workers and peasants. It is significant that it was precisely at the time of the triumph of Fascism that Gramsci devoted himself to the study of the Southern Question and wrote his famous article showing that decisive changes in the social and political structure of the country could only come about as a result of united action by the industrial workers of the North and the peasants of the South.

It was while Gramsci was devoting all his energies to the development of this new movement that he was arrested.

# TWO EDITORIALS FROM *ORDINE NUOVO*

## I

IN this issue we begin the publication of a brief study of Leonardo da Vinci by Comrade Aldo Oberdorfer of Trieste, written on the occasion of da Vinci's fourth centenary to be celebrated this year. We feel sure our readers and friends will not be surprised, as this represents not a failure to live up to our purpose but a partial fulfilment of the aims we made clear from the start.

On other occasions we have already set out what we believe a paper, a Communist cultural review, should be. Such a paper must aim to become, in miniature, complete in itself, and, even though it may be unable to satisfy all the intellectual needs of the nucleus of men who read and support it, who live a part of their lives around it, and who impart to it some of their own life, it must strive to be the kind of journal in which everyone will find things that interest and move him, that will lighten the daily burden of work, economic struggle and political discussion. At the least, the journal should encourage the complete development of one's mental capacities for a higher and fuller life, richer in harmony and in ideological aims, and should be a stimulus for the development of one's own personality. Why cannot we ourselves, with our modest forces, begin the work of the education system, the education system of the future among the youth, who support us and look to us with so much faith and expectation? Because the socialist education system when it emerges will of necessity emerge as a complete system whose goal it will be to embrace quickly all branches of human knowledge. This will be a practical necessity and an intellectual requirement. Are there not already workers to whom the class struggle has given a new sense of dignity and liberty who—when they hear the poets' songs and the names of artists and thinkers—ask bitterly: "Why haven't we, too, been taught these things?" But they console themselves: "Schools, as organised over the last ten years, as organised today by the ruling classes, teach little or nothing." The aim is to meet educational needs by different means: freely, through spontaneous relations between men moved by a common desire to improve themselves. Why couldn't a paper become the centre for one of these groups? In this field, too, the bourgeois régime is on the verge of bankruptcy. From its hands, calloused from their sole work of accumulating private wealth, the torch of science and the sacred lamp of life have fallen. Ours is the task of taking them up, ours the task of making them glow with new light.

In the accumulation of ideas transmitted to us by a millenium of work and thought there are elements which have eternal value, which cannot and must not perish. The loss of consciousness of these values is one of the most serious signs of degradation brought about by the bourgeois régime; to them everything becomes an object of trade and a weapon of war.

The proletariat, having conquered social power, will have to take on the work of reconquest, to restore in full for itself and all humanity the devastated realm of the spirit. This is what the Russian workers, guided by Maxim Gorky, are doing today; this must begin to be done wherever the proletariat is approaching the maturity necessary for social change. The decay at the top must be replaced by new, stronger life from below.

*23 August 1919*

## II

A number of comrades from Turin and the Piedmont region (where our review is especially circulated), inform us that the propaganda work they have engaged in for spreading *Ordine Nuovo* among factory and farm workers is not producing the lasting results which they had hoped to achieve because many comrades find the articles we publish "difficult". From our conversations with these friends we have come to the following conclusions: "psychologically", the period of elementary or so-called "evangelistic" propaganda has passed. The basic ideas of communism have been assimilated by even the most backward elements of the working class. It is astonishing how much the war has contributed to this, army life as well as the brass hats' systematic and savage anti-communist propaganda, which hammered into even the most resistant minds the elementary terms (words, expressions, language) used in the ideological arguments between capitalist and proletariat. First principles must now be taken as understood. We must now turn from the "evangelistic" phase to criticism and reconstruction. Communist experience in Russia and Hungary irresistibly claims our attention. We are avid for information, logical explanations (Are we in Italy ready? Shall we be equal to our task? What errors can we avoid?); we are eager for criticism, criticism, criticism, and for practical experimental ideas. But here the paucity of political education, or rather "constitutional" experience, among the Italian people is revealed. The parliament has always been a dead thing and in Italy there have never taken place, as in England and France, great battles between the popular State institutions (chamber of deputies, local bodies, etc.), and the institutions representing the crown or the most conservative classes (the senate, judiciary, executive).

The crisis through which the Italian proletariat is struggling, caught between the passionate desire to learn and the inability to satisfy this desire individually, must and can be resolved. And it can and must be resolved by methods suited to the workers and peasants, by Communist methods, by the methods of the Soviets. The winning of the eight-hour day leaves a margin of leisure time which must be devoted to cultural work in common. It is essential to convince the workers and peasants that it is above all in their own interest to submit to the permanent discipline of education and to create a conception of their own of the world and the complex and intricate system of human relations, both economic and spiritual, which shapes social life on the globe. These proletarian cultural soviets should be established by friends of *Ordine Nuovo* within workmen's circles and youth groups; they should become the focal point of concrete and realisable Communist education. In them, local and regional problems should be studied; persons should be found who can compile statistics on industrial and agricultural problems in order to determine urgent needs, and also to gain some knowledge of the psychology of small producers, etc.

Let comrades reflect on these considerations. In addition to generous heroism, the revolution also and especially needs painstaking, persistent and persevering work.

*12 July 1919*

# THE PROGRAMME OF *ORDINE NUOVO*

WHEN in April, 1919 we decided—in groups of threes, fours and fives—to begin publication of this review, *Ordine Nuovo* (and the reports must still exist—yes, the reports! because they were drawn up and fair copies were made for history's sake!) not one of us (perhaps just one!) thought in terms of changing the world, of renewing the hearts and minds of masses of human beings, or dreamed of a new era in history. Not one of us (perhaps there was one who dreamed of 6,000 subscribers within a few months) nursed rosy illusions about the success of the enterprise.

Who were we? What did we represent? Of what new idea were we the heralds? Alas, in those meetings of ours the only unifying sentiment arose out of a vague passion for a vague proletarian culture. We wanted to act, act, act. Plunged into the turbulence of those first months following the Armistice when the collapse of Italian society seemed imminent, we felt anguished and disoriented. Alas! The only new idea put forward in those meetings of ours was stifled. One of us who was a technician said: "It is essential to study factory organisation as an instrument of production. We must devote all our attention to capitalist systems of production and organisation and we must work to concentrate the attention of the working class and the Party on this objective." Another, who was concerned with the organisation of men, the history of men, the psychology of the working class, said: "It is necessary to study what is happening among the working masses. Does there exist in Italy a working-class institution at all comparable to, or of the nature of, the Soviets? Anything which gives us the authority to state: 'The Soviet is a universal form, not a Russian, and exclusively Russian, institution. Wherever proletarians are struggling for industrial autonomy, the Soviet is the form through which the working class manifests its desire to emancipate itself.' Is there in Italy, or in Turin, the germ, the feeblest wish for, or even any fear of government by Soviets?" This other, who had been impressed by the question fired point blank at him by a Polish comrade "Why is it that no congress of Factory Committees has ever been held in Italy?" used to answer his own questions in those meetings. "Yes, there is in Italy, in Turin, the germ of a workers' government, the germ of a Soviet. It is the Factory Committees. Let us study this workers' institution, investigate it. Let us also study the capitalist factory, but not as an organisation for material production which would require specialised knowledge we do not possess. Let us study the capitalist factory as a necessary framework for the working class, as a political organism, as the 'national territory' of workers' self government." That idea was new. It was precisely Comrade Tasca who rejected it.

What did Comrade Tasca want? He was opposed to starting any propaganda directly among the workers. He wanted an agreement with the secretaries of the federations and the trade unions; he wanted a meeting of these secretaries to be called, and a plan for an official campaign to be set up. In this way the *Ordine Nuovo* group would have been reduced to the level of an irresponsible clique of upstarts and lone wolves. . . .

What was *Ordine Nuovo* in its first issues? It was an anthology, nothing more; a review which could have come out of Naples, Caltanisetta or Brindisi. It was a journal of abstract culture and abstract information, with a propensity for publishing blood-curdling little stories and well-intentioned woodcuts. This is what *Ordine Nuovo* was—disorganised, the product of mediocre intellectualism clumsily seeking an intellectual platform and a path to action. This was *Ordine Nuovo* launched after the April, 1919 meetings, meetings duly recorded, meetings in which Comrade Tasca dismissed (because it didn't conform to the good traditions of the peaceful well-behaved family of Italian socialism) the proposal that we devote our energies to the discovery of a tradition of Soviets within the Italian working class, to seeking out the thread of real Italian revolutionary spirit—real because it coincides with a universal spirit in the workers' international, because it is the product of a real historical situation, because it is the result of the working class's own development.

We—Togliatti and I—plotted an editorial *coup d'état*. The problem of the Factory Committees was explained clearly in Number 7 of the review. A few nights before writing the article I had discussed the line of the piece with Comrade Terracini and he expressed his full agreement with it both in theory and practice. The article, with Terracini's approval and Togliatti's collaboration, was published and what we had anticipated came to pass. We—Togliatti, Terracini and I—were invited to hold discussions in educational circles, at meetings of factory workers, and we were invited by the Factory Committees to discussions in closed meetings of activists and dues-collectors. We went on. The problem of the development of the Factory Committees became the central problem, it became the *idea* of *Ordine Nuovo*; it was put forward as the fundamental problem of the workers' revolution and of proletarian "freedom". *Ordine Nuovo* for us and for those who followed us, became the "paper of the Factory Councils".

The workers loved *Ordine Nuovo* (this we can state with inner satisfaction), and why did they love *Ordine Nuovo*? Because in the articles of the journal they found something of themselves, their own better selves; because they felt that the articles in it were permeated with their own spirit of self searching: "How can we free ourselves? How can we realise ourselves?" Because the articles in *Ordine Nuovo* were not of cold intellectual construction but flowed out of our own discussions with the best workers and set forth the feelings, wishes, real passions of the Turin working class of which we had partaken and which we had stimulated. And also because the articles in *Ordine Nuovo* were almost a "putting into action" of real events, seen as forces in a process of inner liberation and as the working class's own expression of itself. That is why the workers loved *Ordine Nuovo*, and that is how the idea of *Ordine Nuovo* developed. . . .

. . . Since Comrade Tasca did not participate in this experience and was in fact hostile to its happening at all, the significance of the Factory Councils, in terms of their historical and organic development, escaped him. . . . For Tasca, the problem of the Factory Councils was simply a mathematical one—how to organise immediately the *whole* class of Italian workers and peasants. In one of his sharp polemics, Tasca writes treating the Communist Party, the Trade Unions and the Factory Councils on one level; in another, he shows that he has not understood the meaning of the "voluntary" character which *Ordine Nuovo* ascribes to party organisations and trade unions, differentiating these from the factory councils which are assumed to be a form of "historical" association only comparable to that of the present day bourgeois state. In *Ordine Nuovo*'s view, a view developed around a concept—the concept of liberty (and concretely developed, on the level of the actual making of history, around the hypothesis of autonomous revolutionary action by the working class), the factory council is an institution of a "public" character while the Party and the trade unions are associations of a "private" nature.

In the Factory Councils the worker, because of his very nature, plays the rôle of producer as a result of his position and function in society, in the same way as the citizen plays a rôle in the democratic parliamentary state. In the Party and trade unions, the worker plays his rôle "voluntarily", signing a written pledge—a contract which he can tear up at any moment. The Party and the trade unions, because of this "voluntary" character, because of their "contractual" nature, are not to be confused with the councils which are representative institutions and do not develop mathematically but morphologically, and in their higher forms tend to give a proletarian meaning to the apparatus, created by the capitalist for the purpose of extracting profit, of production and exchange. The development of higher forms of organisation of the councils was therefore not raised by *Ordine Nuovo* in the political terminology of society divided into social classes, but with the reference to industrial organisation.

In *Ordine Nuovo*'s view, the system of councils cannot be expressed by the term "association" or words of similar meaning, but can only be represented by reproducing for a whole industrial centre the complex industrial relationships which bind one team of workers to another, one department to another, in one factory. The Turin example was a model for us and thus in one article it was taken as the historic forge of the Italian Communist revolution. In a factory, workers are producers because they work together to produce the manufactured object, and are deployed in a manner precisely determined by industrial techniques which are (in a certain sense) independent of the system by which the value of the things produced is appropriated. All the workers in an automobile factory, whether sheetmetal workers, vehicle builders, electricians, woodworkers, etc., take on the character of producers because they are all equally necessary and indispensable to the automobile factory, and inasmuch as they are bound together industrially they constitute a necessary and absolutely indivisible historic organism. Turin, as a city, developed historically in this way. Because of the transfer of the capital to Florence and then Rome, and because the Italian state was first formed as an outgrowth of Piedmont, Turin lost its petit-bourgeois class, sections of which provided the personnel for the new Italian state apparatus. But the transfer of the capital and the impoverishment of this typical element of all modern cities did not bring about a decline; the city, in fact, began to develop again and the new development went hand in hand with the development of the engineering industry, with the Fiat factories. Turin gave the new state its class of petit-bourgeois intellectuals; and the development of the capitalist economy, ruining the small-scale industries and artisans of the Italian nation, at the same time caused the growth in Turin of a compact proletarian mass which gives the city its present character, perhaps unique in all Europe. The city developed around the central pattern which it still retains, organised naturally around the industry which "governs" the whole urban growth of the city and regulates its outlets. Turin is an automobile city in the same way that Vercelli is organised around rice, the Caucasus around petrol, South Wales around coal, etc. As in a factory, where workers assume a pattern governed by the production of a given object which unites and organises metal-workers and woodworkers, constructional workers, electricians, etc., so in a city, the proletariat adopts patterns determined by the prevalent industry which dominates the whole urban life. So, on a national scale, a people adopts the pattern laid down by its exports, by the real contribution the nation makes to the economic life of the world.

Comrade Tasca, a very inattentive reader of *Ordine Nuovo*, stated none of these theoretical explanations, which in any case were no more than a translation, in terms of Italian historical reality, of the idea developed by Comrade Lenin in several writings published by *Ordine Nuovo*, and of the ideas of the American theorist of the revolutionary syndicalist association, the I.W.W., the Marxist Daniel de Leon. In point of fact, Comrade Tasca at one point interpreted the symbols of mass production expressed by words like rice, wood, sulphur, etc., in a merely "commercial" book-keeping sense. Again, he asks what relationship there could be between the councils. In a third point, he ascribes the origin of the ideas set forth in *Ordine Nuovo* to the Proudhonian concept of the workshop destroying the government, although in that same issue of *Ordine Nuovo* of June 5th which carried the piece on the Factory Councils and the comments by the Trades Union Congress, there was also printed an extract from Marx on the Paris Commune in which Marx clearly recognises the industrial character of the communist society of producers. In this work by Marx, Lenin and de Leon found the basic inspiration for their ideas, and it was on these extracts that the *Ordine Nuovo* articles were prepared and written. Again, and precisely because it was around this issue that the polemic started, Comrade Tasca proved his reading to be superficial and without understanding of the ideological and historical substance which it contained.

The comments made at the Trades Union Congress on Comrade Tasca's attempt to influence the vote on an executive motion, were dictated by the desire to keep *Ordine Nuovo's* programme intact. The factory councils have their own rules; they cannot and must not accept trade union rules because it is precisely their aim to remodel these fundamentally. Similarly, the Factory Councils' movement wants workers' representatives to come directly from the masses and to be bound to the masses by an imperative mandate. Comrade Tasca's speech at a workers' congress, without a mandate from anyone, on a problem of concern to the whole mass of workers and the solution of which should unite the masses, was so much opposed to the ideas of *Ordine Nuovo* that a sharp reply was perfectly justified and completely deserved.

*ORDINE NUOVO*
*August 1920*

# THE SOUTHERN QUESTION

THE incentive for these notes comes from the publication in the *Quarto Stato* of September 18th of an article on the southern question, signed *Ulenspiegel*, to which the editors of the review have added a somewhat ridiculous preface. *Ulenspiegel* comments, in his article, on a recent book by Guido Dorso (*La Rivoluzione Meridionale*) and refers to the opinion which Dorso has expressed on our party's position on the question of the South; in their preface the editors of *Quarto Stato*, who proclaim that they are "young men who are *perfectly* well acquainted in its *general lines* (sic) with the southern problem", protest collectively against any "merit" being allowed to the Communist Party. So far so good; the young men of the *Quarto Stato* type have, at every time and place, sustained on paper their very different opinions and made their protests without the paper rebelling. But then these "young men" add in their text: "We have not forgotten the magic formula of the Turin Communists which was: divide the estates among the rural proletariat. That formula is worlds removed from any sane, realistic view of the southern problem." And so it is necessary to straighten things out, since the only "magic" thing that exists is the effrontery and dilletante superficiality of the "young" writers of the *Quarto Stato*.

The "magic formula" is a complete invention. And the "young men" of the *Quarto Stato* must have a very low opinion of their highly intellectual readers if it is their habit to turn truth upside down with such wordy pomposity. Here, indeed, is an extract from *Ordine Nuovo* for January 3rd, 1920, in which the viewpoint of the Turin Communists is summarised:

"The bourgeoisie of the North has subjected southern Italy and the Islands and reduced them to the status of exploited colonies; the proletariat of the North, in emancipating itself from capitalist enslavement, will emancipate the peasant masses of the South who are chained to the banks and the parasitic industrialism of the North. The economic regeneration of the peasants must not be sought in dividing up the uncultivated and badly cultivated lands, but in solidarity with the industrial proletariat, which needs in its turn the solidarity of the peasants, and which is greatly interested in seeing that capitalism is not reborn economically from landed property, and also that southern Italy and the Islands shall not become a military base for capitalist counter-revolution. In imposing workers' control over industry, the proletariat will direct industry towards the production of agricultural machinery for the peasants, of textiles and shoes for the peasants, and of electrical energy for the peasants; it will prevent industry and the banks carrying out any further exploitation of the peasants and chaining them like slaves to their strongboxes. In breaking up the autocracy in the factories, destroying the oppressive apparatus of the capitalist State, and installing the workers' State, which will subject capitalists to the laws of useful work, the workers will break all the chains which bind the peasant to poverty and despair; in installing the workers' dictatorship, having in its hands industry and the banks, the proletariat will direct the enormous power of state organisation towards helping the peasants in their struggle against the landowners, against nature and against poverty; it will give credit to the peasants, institute co-operatives, guarantee personal security and property against plunderers, and carry out public expenditure for development and irrigation. It will do all this because it is in its own interests to increase agricultural production, to win and conserve the solidarity of the peasant masses, and because it is in its own interest to direct industrial production towards the useful aim of peace and brotherhood between town and country, between North and South."

This was written in January, 1920. Seven years have passed and we are seven years older politically as well; one or two concepts could be expressed better today—the period immediately following the conquest of the State, characterised by simple workers' control over industry, could and should be better distinguished from the later periods. But what is important to note here is that the fundamental concept of the Turin Communists was not the "magic formula" of the division of the estates, but that of the political alliance between the workers of the North and the peasants of the South to overthrow the state power of the bourgeoisie: not only this, but the Turin Communists themselves (who, however, supported the division of the lands as subordinate to united class action) warned against any illusions of miraculous results from the mechanical partition of the estates. The article of January 3rd continues: "What does the poor peasant gain by invading uncultivated or badly cultivated lands? Without machines, without a dwelling on his place of work, without credit with which to await the harvest, without co-operative institutions which might acquire the harvest itself (if he lives to see the harvest without first having hanged himself from the sturdiest tree of the woodlands or the least diseased fig-tree of the uncultivated lands), and save him from the clutches of the usurers, what can a poor peasant gain from the invasion?" And nevertheless we favoured a very realistic and not at all "magic" formula of the land for the peasants; but we wanted it to be realised inside the framework of the general revolutionary action of the two allied classes, under the leadership of the industrial proletariat. The writers of the *Quarto Stato* have simply invented the "magic formula" which they attribute to the Turin Communists, thus showing that they are about as reliable as hack journalists and as scrupulous as small town intellectuals: even these are political elements who carry some weight.

In the proletarian camp, the Turin Communists have one undeniable "merit": they have brought the southern question to the attention of the vanguard of the working class, formulating it as one of the essential problems of the national policy of the revolutionary proletariat. In this sense they have contributed practically to bringing the southern question out of its indistinct, intellectualistic, so-called "concretist" phase, and made it enter a new phase. The revolutionary workers of Turin and Milan have become the protagonists of the southern question, and no longer Giustino Fortunato, Gaetano Salvemini, Eugenio Azimonti, Arturo Labriola, to mention only the names of the saints dear to the "young men" of the *Quarto Stato*.

The Turin Communists posed to themselves concretely the question of the "hegemony of the proletariat", in other words, of the social basis of the proletarian dictatorship and the Workers' State. The proletariat can become the leading and ruling class to the extent to which it succeeds in creating a system of class alliances which enables it to mobilise the majority of the working population against capitalism and the bourgeois State; this means, in Italy, in the actual relations existing in Italy, to the extent to which it succeeds in obtaining the consent of the large peasant masses. But the peasant question in Italy is historically determined, and is not "the peasant and agrarian question in general"; in Italy the peasant question has, through the determined Italian tradition, through the determined development of Italian history, assumed two typical and peculiar forms, the southern question and the Vatican question. To conquer the majority of the peasant masses means, therefore, for the Italian proletariat, to make these two questions its own from a social point of view, to understand the class exigencies that they represent, to incorporate these exigencies into its own revolutionary programme of transition, to place these exigencies among its aims in the struggle.

The first problem to be solved, for the Turin Communists, was that of modifying the political orientation and general ideology of the proletariat itself, as a national element which lives inside the complex of the life of the State and undergoes unconsciously the influence of the schools, of the newspapers, of the bourgeois tradition. It is well known what ideology is propagated through the multifarious forms of bourgeois propaganda among the masses of the North: the South is a lead weight which impedes a more rapid civil development of Italy; the southerners are biologically inferior beings, semi-barbarians or complete barbarians by natural destiny; if the South is backward, the fault is not to be found in the capitalist system or in any other historical cause, but is the fault of nature which has made the southerner lazy, incapable, criminal, barbarous, moderating his stepmother's fate by the purely individual outbursts of great geniuses, who are like solitary palms in an arid and sterile desert. The Socialist Party was very largely the vehicle of this bourgeois ideology among the northern proletariat; the Socialist Party gave its blessing to the whole "*southernist*" literature of the clique of so-called positivist writers like Ferri, Sergi, Niceforo, Orano and their minor followers, who in articles, sketches, stories, novels, books of impressions and memoirs repeated in various forms the same refrain; once again "science" had turned to crushing the wretched and the exploited, but this time it was cloaked in socialist colours, pretending to be the science of the proletariat.

The Turin Communists reacted energetically against this ideology, at Turin itself, where the tales and descriptions of the veterans of the war against "brigandage" in the South and the Islands had most influenced tradition and the popular spirit. They reacted energetically, in practical ways, succeeding in obtaining concrete results of the greatest historical importance, succeeding in creating, actually in Turin, the embryo of what will be the solution of the southern problem.

In fact, already before the war, there had occurred in Turin an episode which potentially contained all the action and propaganda developed in the post-war period by the Communists. When in 1914, through the death of Pilade Gay, Ward IV of the city became vacant and the question of the new candidate was posed, a group of Socialists to which belonged the future editors of *Ordine Nuovo*, aired the project of presenting Gaetano Salvemini as candidate. Salvemini was then the most advanced spokesman, in a radical sense, of the peasant masses of the South. He was outside the Socialist Party, and was moreover conducting a most lively and dangerous campaign against the Socialist Party, since his assertions and accusations had become among the working masses of the South a cause of hatred not only against Treves, Turati and d'Aragona but against the industrial proletariat as a whole. (Many of the bullets which the royal guards fired in '19, '20, '21, '22 against the workers were cast out of the same lead which had been used to print Salvemini's articles.) Nevertheless the Turin group wanted to make a demonstration around the name of Salvemini, in the sense that was put to Salvemini by Comrade Ottavio Pastore who came to Florence to get his consent for the canditature. "The workers of Turin want to elect a deputy for the Apulian peasants. The workers of Turin know that in the general elections of 1913 the overwhelming majority of peasants of Molfetta and Bitonto supported Salvemini; the administrative pressure of the Giolitti government and the violence of the gangs and the police prevented the Apulian peasants expressing themselves. The workers of Turin do not ask for pledges from Salvemini, neither of Party programme nor of discipline within the Parliamentary group; once elected Salvemini will answer to the Apulian peasants, not to the workers of Turin, who will carry on their propaganda according to their principles and will not be at all committed by the political activity of Salvemini."

Salvemini was unwilling to accept the candidature, although he was shaken and even moved by the proposal (at that time they were not yet talking of Communist "perfidy" and people were behaving honestly and pleasantly); he proposed Mussolini as candidate and pledged himself to come to Turin to help the Socialist Party in the election battle. In fact he held two great meetings at the *Camera del Lavoro* (the central trade union offices of the city, *Trans.*), and in the *Piazza Statuto*, where the masses saw and applauded in him the representative of the southern peasants who were oppressed and exploited in even more bestial and hateful ways than the proletariat of the North.

The orientation, potentially contained in this episode which developed no further only because of Salvemini's decision, was taken up again and applied by the Communists in the post-war period. We wish to recall the most salient and symptomatic facts.

In 1919 the "Young Sardinia" association was formed, the beginning and forerunner of what later became the Sardinian Party of Action. "Young Sardinia" set itself to unite all the Sardinians on the island and the mainland into a regional *bloc* capable of exercising a useful pressure on the government in order to obtain the fulfilment of the promises made to the soldiers during the war; the organiser of "Young Sardinia" on the mainland was one Professor Nurra, a socialist, who is very likely today one of the "young men" of the *Quarto Stato* who every week discover a new horizon to explore. Lawyers, professors and functionaries joined with the enthusiasm aroused by every new possibility of fishing for titles and medals. The foundation meeting, called at Turin for Sardinians living in Piedmont, had an imposing success to judge by the number who took part. Poor people were in the majority, common folk without any distinguishing qualifications, factory labourers, small pensioners, ex-carabinieri, ex-prison-guards, ex-customs-officials who carried on various small businesses; all were enthusiastic at the idea of finding themselves among compatriots, of hearing speeches about their country to which they continued to feel tied by innumerable threads of relationship, friendship, memories, suffering and hope—the hope of returning to their country, but to a more prosperous and richer country which offered prospects of livelihood, even though of a modest kind.

The Sardinian Communists, precisely eight in number, went to the meeting, presented their motion to the president, and asked to be allowed to speak to it. After the inflammatory and rhetorical discourse of the official speaker, adorned with all the frills of provincial oratory, after the audience had wept at the memory of past sufferings and of the blood spilt in the war by the Sardinian regiments, and had worked themselves up to a frenzy at the idea of a compact *bloc* of all the noble sons of Sardinia, it was very difficult to "put across" the opposition motion; the most optimistic prophesies were, if not for a lynching, at least for a walk to the police station after being saved from the consequences of the "noble scorn of the crowd". This speech, if it aroused enormous surprise, was however, listened to with attention, and once the spell had been broken, rapidly, though methodically, drove home its revolutionary lesson. The dilemma—"Are you poor devils from Sardinia in favour of a *bloc* with the gentry of Sardinia who have ruined you and are the local overseers of capitalist exploitation, or are you for a *bloc* with the revolutionary workers of the mainland who want to overthrow all exploitation and emancipate all the oppressed?"—this dilemma was made to penetrate into the brains of those present. The vote was a tremendous success: on the one side a small group of overdressed ladies, high-hatted officials, professional people, all livid from rage or fear, and with about forty policemen forming an outer rim of consent; and on the other side the whole multitude of poor devils and women charming in their Sunday dresses, supporting the tiny group of Communists. One hour later at the *Camera del Lavoro* the Sardinian Socialist Educational Circle was set up with 256 members; the constitution of "Young Sardinia" was referred back *sine die* and never came into effect.

This was the political basis of the campaign carried on among the soldiers of the Sassari Brigade, a brigade of almost entirely provincial composition. The Sassari Brigade had taken part in the suppression of the insurrectionary movement at Turin in August, 1917; they were sure that it would never fraternise with the workers, on account of the memories of hatred which every repression leaves with the people even against the material instruments of the repression, and which it leaves with the soldiers, who remember their comrades killed by the insurgents. The Brigade was welcomed by a crowd of ladies and gentlemen who offered flowers, cigars and fruit to the troops. The state of mind of the soldiers is illustrated by this story of a leather worker of

Sassari, charged with the first soundings of propaganda: "I approached a bivouac in Piazza X (the Sardinian soldiers in the first days camped in the squares as if in a conquered city), and spoke to a young peasant who had welcomed me cordially because I was from Sassari like him.

" 'What have you come to do in Turin?'

" 'We have come to fire on the gentry who are on strike.'

" 'But it is not gentry who are on strike, it is the poor people and the workers.'

" 'Here they are all gentry: they all wear collars and ties; they earn thirty *lire* a day. I know poor people and how they dress; at Sassari, yes, there are many poor people; all we countryfolk are poor and we earn one and a half *lire* a day.'

" 'But I too am a worker and I am poor.'

" 'You are poor because you are Sardinian.'

" 'But if I go on strike with the others, will you fire on me?'

"The soldier reflected a little, then putting his hand on my shoulder said: 'Listen, when you go on strike with the others, stay at home!' "

The great majority of the Brigade, which only included a small number of mining workers from the Iglesias basin, were in this frame of mind. Still, after a few months, on the eve of the general strike of July 20th–21st, the Brigade was removed far from Turin, the old soldiers were sent on leave and the formation divided into three: a third went to Aosta, a third to Trieste, and a third to Rome. The Brigade was made to leave suddenly, at night; no elegant crowd cheered them at the station; their songs, if they were still martial songs, no longer had the same content as when they arrived.

Were these events without consequence? No, they had results which still persist today and continue to operate in the heart of the masses. In a flash they lit up brains which had never thought in such a way before and which remained impressed and radically changed. Our records have been dispersed, and many papers destroyed by ourselves in order not to provoke arrests and persecutions. But we remember tens of thousands of letters from Sardinia which reached the editors of *Avanti!*; often collective letters, often letters signed by all the ex-combatants of the Sassari from a certain village. Through uncontrolled and uncontrollable ways our political standpoint was propagated; the formation of the Sardinian Party of Action was strongly influenced at the rank and file level, and it would be possible to recall in this connection episodes rich in content and significance.

The last recorded repercussion of this action took place in 1922, when, with the same purpose as the Sassari Brigade, three hundred *carabinieri* of the *Legione di Cagliari* were sent to Turin. At the editorial office of *Ordine Nuovo* we received a declaration of principle signed by a large number of these *carabinieri*. This echoed entirely our own assessment of the southern problem, it was a decisive proof of the correctness of our line.

The proletariat had to make this its own line in order to give it political effect: that is understood. No mass action is possible unless the mass itself is convinced of the ends it wants to reach and the methods to be applied. The proletariat, in order to be able to rule as a class, must rid itself of all corporative hangovers, of all syndicalist prejudices and incrustations. What does this mean? That not only must the distinctions which exist between trades and crafts be overcome, but that it is necessary, in order to win the trust and consent of the peasants and of the semi-proletarian categories in the cities, to overcome prejudices and conquer certain egoistic traits which can exist and do exist in the working class as such, even when craft particularism has disappeared from its midst. The metalworkers, the joiners, the builders, etc., must not only think as proletarians and no longer as metalworkers, joiners or builders, but they must take a step forward: they must think as members of a class which aims at leading the peasants and the intellectuals, of a class which can conquer and can build socialism only if aided and followed by the great majority of these social strata. If it does not do this, the proletariat does not become a leading class, and these strata, who in Italy represent the majority of the population, remain under bourgeois leadership, and give the State the possibility of resisting and weakening the proletarian attack.

Well then: what has taken place in the field of the southern question shows that the proletariat has understood these duties. Two events should be recalled: one at Turin, the other at Reggio Emilia; that is to say in the citadel of reformism, of class corporativism, of working-class protectionism quoted as an example by the "Southernists", in their propaganda among the peasants of the South.

After the occupation of the factories the directors of Fiat proposed to the workers that the factory should be carried on as a co-operative. Naturally, the reformists were in favour An industrial crisis was looming ahead. The prospect of unemployment brought anguish to working-class homes. If Fiat became a co-operative, a certain security of employment could result, especially for the most politically active workers, who were convinced that they were destined to be laid off.

The Socialist organisation, guided by the Communists, took a firm stand. They said to the workers:

"A great co-operative enterprise like Fiat can be taken over by the workers only if the workers have decided to enter into the system of bourgeois political power which today rules Italy. The proposal of the Fiat directors is part of Giolitti's political plan. In what does this plan consist? The bourgeoisie, already before the war, was unable to govern peacefully any more. The insurrection of the Sicilian peasants in 1894 and the insurrection at Milan in 1898 were the *experimentum crucis* of the Italian bourgeoisie. After the ten bloody years of 1890-1900 the bourgeoisie had to renounce its over-exclusive, over-violent, over-direct dictatorship: the peasants of the South and the workers of the North were rising *simultaneously*, even if not in a co-ordinated manner, against them. In the new century the ruling class began a new policy, that of class alliances, of political *blocs* of classes, i.e. of bourgeois democracy. It had to choose: either a rural democracy, that is, an alliance with the southern peasants, a policy of tariff freedom, of universal suffrage, of administrative decentralisation, of low prices for industrial products, or an industrial *bloc* of capitalists and workers, without universal suffrage, for tariff protection, for the maintenance of state centralisation (the expression of bourgeois rule over the peasants, especially in the South and the Islands), for a re-formist policy in wages and freedom for trade unions. Not by chance it chose this second solution; Giolitti embodied the bourgeois rule, the Socialist Party became the instrument of Giolittian policy. If you look into it well you see that in the ten years 1900-1910 there took place the most radical crises in the Socialist and workers movement: the masses reacted spontaneously against the policy of the reformist leaders. Syndicalism was born, which is the instinctive, elementary, primitive but healthy expression of the working-class reaction against the *bloc* with the bourgeoisie and in favour of a *bloc* with the peasants, and in the *first place with the peasants of the South*. Just so: moreover, in a certain sense, syndicalism is a weak attempt by the southern peasants, represented by their most advanced intellectuals, to lead the proletariat. Who constitutes the leading nucleus of Italian syndicalism? What is the essential ideology of Italian syndicalism? The leading nucleus of syndicalism is almost exclusively made up of southerners: Labriola, Leone, Longobardi, Orano. The essential ideology of syndicalism is a new liberalism, more energetic, more aggressive, more pugnacious than traditional liberalism. If you look into it, you see that there are two fundamental questions over which arise the successive crises of syndicalism and the gradual passing over of syndicalist leaders into the bourgeois camp: emigration and free-trade, two subjects closely linked with the South. The phenomenon of emigration gives rise to the conception of the "proletarian nation" of Enrico Corradini; the Libyan war appears to a whole strata of intellectuals as the beginning of the offensive of the "great proletarian nation" against the capitalistic and plutocratic world. A whole group of syndicalists passed over to nationalism, in fact the Nationalist Party was originally constituted of ex-syndicalist intellectuals (Monicelli, Forges-Davanzati, Maraviglia). Labriola's book *History of Ten Years* (the ten years from 1900 to 1910) is the most typical and characteristic expression of this anti-Giolittian and "southernist" neoliberalism.

"In these ten years capitalism was strengthened and developed, and poured a part of its activity into the Po Valley. A profound change took place among the northern peasants; we saw profound class differentiation occur (the number of farm labourers increased by 50 per cent, according to the figures of the 1911 census), and to this corresponded a re-alignment of political trends and of spiritual standpoints. Christian Democracy and Mussolinism are the two most salient products of the period: the Romagna is the provincial crucible of this new activity; the farm labourer seems to have become the social protagonist in the political battle. Social democracy in its left-wing organisations (the newspaper *L'Azione*, of Cesena), and even Mussolinism fell rapidly under the control of the "southernists". *L'Azione* of Cesena was a provincial edition of Gaetano Salvemini's *Unità*. *Avanti* directed by Mussolini was slowly but surely transformed into a platform for syndicalist and southernist writers. Fancello, Lanzillo, Panunzio, Ciccoti became its assiduous contributors: Salvemini himself did not hide his sympathies for Mussolini, who also became a favourite with Prezzolini's *Voce*. Everyone remembers that in effect, when Mussolini left *Avanti* and the Socialist Party he was surrounded by this cohort of syndicalists and southernists.

"The most noteworthy repercussion of this period in the revolutionary field was the Red Week of June, 1914: the Romagna and the Marches were the centre of Red Week. In the field of bourgeois politics the most noteworthy repercussion was the Gentiloni pact. Since the Socialist Party, through the effect of the agrarian movement on the Po Valley, had returned, after 1910, to intransigent tactics, the industrial *bloc*, supported and represented by Giolitti, lost its efficacy: Giolitti changed his rifle to the other shoulder; for the alliance between bourgeoisie and workers he substituted the alliance between the bourgeoisie and the Catholics, who represent the peasant masses of Northern and Central Italy. As a result of this alliance the Conservative Party of Sonnino came to be completely destroyed, only preserving its smallest cell in Southern Italy around Antonio Salandra. The war and its aftermath have seen the development of a series of molecular processes of the utmost importance in the bourgeois class. Salandra and Nitti were the first two southerners to head the government (not to mention the Sicilians, naturally, like Crispi, who was the most energetic representative of the bourgeois dictatorship in the nineteenth century), and sought to carry into effect the bourgeois industrial-agrarian plan for the South, Salandra in the conservative field, Nitti in the democratic field (both these heads of the government were solidly helped by the *Corriere della Sera*, i.e. by the Lombardy textile industry). Already before the war, Salandra sought to redirect the technical forces of state organisation in favour of the South, and sought to substitute for the Giolittian personnel of the State a new personnel which would embody the new course of bourgeois policy. You remember the campaign conducted in *La Stampa* especially in 1917-1918 in favour of close collaboration between the Giolittians and the Socialists in order to prevent the 'Apulianisation' of the State: that campaign was conducted in *La Stampa* by Francesco Ciccotti; in other words, it was precisely an expression of the existing

agreement between Giolitti and the reformists. The question was not
a small one and the Giolittians, in their obstinate resistance, reached
the point of exceeding the limits allowed to a party of the big bourgeoisie and went as far as those demonstrations of anti-patriotism and
defeatism which are in the memory of all. Giolitti is again in power
today, the big bourgeoisie is again trusting him, as a result of the panic
which seized them in face of the impetuous movement of the popular
masses. Giolitti wants to domesticate the workers of Turin. He has
defeated them twice: in last April's strike and in the occupation of
the factories, both times with the help of the General Confederation
of Labour, that is, of corporative reformism. He now thinks that he
can bring them into the framework of the bourgeois state system. In
fact what will happen if the Fiat workers accept the proposal of the
Directors? The present shares will become debentures; the co-operative will have to pay a fixed dividend to the holders of debentures,
whatever the state of business. The Fiat concern will be enmeshed in
every way by the credit institutions, which remain in the hands of the
bourgeoisie, which has an interest in reducing the workers to its will.
The workers will necessarily have to tie themselves to the State,
which 'will come to the help of the workers' through working-class
deputies, through the subordination of the working-class political
party to government policy. That is Giolitti's plan in its full application. The Turin proletariat will no longer exist as an independent
class but only as an appendage of the bourgeois State. Class co-operation will have triumphed, but the proletariat will have lost its position
and its rôle as leader and guide; it will appear to the mass of poorer
workers as a privileged group, it will appear to the peasants as an
exploiter like the bourgeoisie, since the bourgeoisie, as it has always
done, will present the privileged nucleus of workers to the peasant
masses as the sole cause of their sufferings and of their poverty."

The Fiat workers accepted our point of view almost unanimously,
and the Directors' proposal was rejected. But this single experiment
could not be sufficient. The Turin proletariat, by a whole series of
actions, had shown that they had reached a very high level of political
maturity and capacity. The technical and supervisory grades and
factory clerks, in 1919, were able to better their conditions only because
they were supported by the workers. In order to break up the agitation

of the higher grades, the industrialists proposed to the workers that they should themselves nominate, by election, new foremen and new superintendents; the workers rejected the proposal, although they had several reasons for conflict with the supervisory grades who had always been an instrument of the bosses for repression and victimisation. Then the newspapers conducted a furious campaign to isolate these grades, drawing attention to their very high salaries which reached up to 7,000 *lire* a month. The technical workers helped the agitation of the manual workers, who only in this way were able to impose their will: inside the factory all the privileges and exploitation by which the more qualified categories benefited at the cost of the less qualified were swept away. Through this action the proletarian vanguard won for itself the social position of a vanguard: this has been the basis for the development of the Communist Party at Turin. But outside Turin? Very well, we wanted to take the matter outside Turin and precisely to Reggio Emilia, where there used to exist the greatest concentration of reformism and class co-operation.

Reggio Emilia had always been the target of the "southernists". A phrase of Camillo Prampolini: "Italy is divided into Northerners and filthy Southerners",[1] was a most characteristic expression of the violent hatred against the workers of the North among the southerners. At Reggio Emilia a similar question to that at Fiat was presented: a large factory was to pass into the hands of the workers as a co-operative enterprise. The Reggio reformists supported the proposal enthusiastically and trumpeted it around in their newspapers and meetings. A Turin Communist went to Reggio, spoke at a mass meeting in the factory, dealt with the question of the North and the South in all its complexity, and the "miracle" was achieved: the workers by a very large majority rejected the reformist and corporative thesis. It was shown that the reformists did not represent the spirit of the workers of Reggio; they only represented its passive and negative sides. They had succeeded in establishing a political monopoly, in view of the remarkable number of capable organisers and propagandists at their disposal, and therefore in preventing the development and organisation of a

[1] It is impossible to render in English the pun contained in the words 'nordici' and 'sudici'.

revolutionary trend; but the presence of one capable revolutionary was sufficient to put them to flight and reveal that the Reggian workers were brave fighters and not pigs bred on government corn.

In April, 1921, 5,000 revolutionary workers were laid off by Fiat, the Factory Councils were abolished, real wages were reduced. At Reggio Emilia something similar probably happened. The workers, in other words, were defeated. But has their sacrifice been useless? We do not think so: rather are we sure that it has not been useless. It is certainly difficult to draw up a list of mass events to demonstrate the immediate effects of these actions. But as regards the peasants, such lists are always difficult and almost impossible to draw up, especially in the case of the peasant masses of the South.

The South can be described as an area of extreme social disintegration. The peasants who constitute the great majority of the population have no cohesion among themselves. (Naturally it is necessary to make exceptions: Apulia, Sardinia, Sicily, where special conditions exist inside the broad framework of the southern structure.) The society of the South is a great agrarian *bloc* consisting of three social strata: the large, amorphous, scattered peasant masses; the intellectuals of the petty and middle rural bourgeoisie; the big property owners and the top intellectuals. The southern peasants are in perpetual ferment, but as a mass they are incapable of giving a unified expression to their aspirations and their needs. The middle strata of intellectuals receives from the peasants the impulses for its political and ideological activity. The big property owners in the political field and the top intellectuals in the ideological field hold together and dominate, in the last analysis, all this complex of phenomena. As is natural, it is in the ideological field that centralism shows itself with greatest effect and precision. Giustino Fortunato and Benedetto Croce therefore represent the keystones of the southern system and, in a certain sense, are the two greatest figures of Italian reaction.

The southern intellectuals are among the most interesting and important strata in Italian national life. It is sufficient to remember that three-fifths of the State bureaucracy is composed of southerners to be convinced of this. Now, in order to understand the particular psychology of the southern intellectuals it is necessary to take the following facts into account:

1. In every country the stratum of the intellectuals has been radically altered by the development of capitalism. The old type of intellectual was the organising element of a society based predominantly on peasants and artisans; in order to organise the State and to organise trade, the ruling class bred a particular type of intellectual. Industry has introduced a new type of intellectual: the technical organiser, the specialist of applied science. In societies where the economic forces are developed in a capitalist sense to the point of absorbing the major part of national activity, it is this second type of intellectual which has prevailed, with all its characteristics of intellectual order and discipline. But in those countries where agriculture still plays a large and even a preponderant rôle, the old type has remained prevalent, providing most of the State personnel and locally, in the small towns and rural centres, carrying out the function of intermediary between the peasant and the administration in general. In Southern Italy this type predominates, with all its characteristics: democratic in its peasant face, reactionary when its face is turned towards the big property owner and the government, much given to political intrigue, corrupt, disloyal; one would not understand the traditional character of the southern political parties unless one took into account the character of this social stratum.

2. The southern intellectual comes mainly from a class which is still widespread in the South: the rural bourgeois, that is, the small and middle land-owner who is not a peasant, who does not work the land, who would be ashamed to carry on agriculture, but who wishes to extract from the little land he has, let out on lease or in *mezzadria semplice*,[1] enough to live comfortably, to send his sons to the university or the seminary, to provide dowries for his daughters whom he hopes to marry to State officials or civil servants. From this class the intellectuals derive a strong aversion for the peasant labourer whom they look on as a living machine that must be worked to the bone and can easily be replaced in view of over-population: they also inherit an atavistic and instinctive feeling of crazy fear of the peasant and his destructive violence, and hence a habit of refined hypocrisy and a most refined skill in deceiving and breaking in the peasant masses.

---

[1] A semi-feudal form of land-holding by which the peasant pays from 40 per cent to 50 per cent of the produce of the land as rent to the landlord.

3. Since the clergy belong to the social group of the intellectuals it is necessary to note the differences in character between the southern clergy as a whole and the northern clergy. The northern priest is usually the son of an artisan or a peasant; he has democratic sentiments and closer ties with the peasant masses; he is morally more correct than the southern priest, who often openly co-habits with a woman, and he therefore exercises a more socially complete spiritual office, that is to say, he is the leader of all family activity. In the North the separation of the Church from the State and the expropriation of ecclesiastical property has been more thoroughgoing than in the South, where the parishes and convents have preserved or reconstituted a good deal of both fixed and moveable property. In the South the priest appears to the peasant: (1) as a bailiff with whom the peasant comes into conflict over the question of rents; (2) as a usurer who demands the highest rates of interest, and plays up religious obligations to secure the payment of rent or interest; (3) as a man who is subject to common passions (women and money) and so spiritually inspires no confidence in either his discretion or impartiality. Confession, therefore, has little significance, and the southern peasant, though often superstitious in a pagan sense, is not priest-ridden. This whole set-up explains why in the South the Popular Party (except in certain zones in Sicily) has comparatively little influence, and possesses no apparatus of institutions and mass organisations. The attitude of the peasant towards the clergy is summed up in the popular saying: "The priest is a priest at the altar; elsewhere he is a man like any other."

The southern peasant is tied to the big landowner through the activity of the intellectual. The peasant movements, in so far as they are not expressed in at least formally autonomous and independent mass organisations (i.e. organisations capable of selecting peasant cadres of peasant origin and of reflecting the differentiations and progress achieved in the movement) always end up by losing themselves in the ordinary forms of the State apparatus—Communes, Provinces, Chamber of Deputies—through the combinations and breaking up of the local parties, which consist of intellectuals but are controlled by the big property owners and their trusted men, like Salandra, Orlando or di Cesaro. The war seemed to introduce a new element into this type of organisation with the ex-servicemen's movement, in which peasant-soldiers and intellectual-officers formed themselves into a more united *bloc* which was to a certain extent antagonistic to the big land-owners. It did not last long and its last remnant is the National Union conceived by Amendola, which still has a glimmer of existence thanks to its antifascism; nevertheless, because there is no tradition of explicit organisation of the democratic intellectuals of the South, even such a grouping as this is significant, since from being a mere trickle it can in different political conditions become a torrent. The only region where the ex-servicemen's movement assumes a clearer outline and is succeeding in creating a more solid social structure is Sardinia. And this is natural: precisely because in Sardinia the class of big landowners is very small, does not carry out any necessary function and does not have the very old cultural and governmental traditions of the main-land South. The pressure from below exercised by the mass of peasants and shepherds is not suffocated by the counterweight of the upper stratum of big proprietors: the leading intellectuals take the whole pressure, and have in some ways moved further forward than the National Union. The Sicilian situation is profoundly different from either Sardinia or the South. The big property-owners there are much more cohesive and resolute than in the mainland South; in addition there exists a certain amount of industry and a highly developed trade (Sicily is the richest region of all the South and is one of the richest in Italy); the upper classes feel strongly their importance in the national life and make it carry weight. Sicily and Piedmont are the two regions which have given the greatest number of political leaders to the Italian State, and are the two regions which have played a prominent rôle since 1870. The Sicilian masses are more advanced than in the South, but progress there has taken on a typically Sicilian form; a Sicilian mass socialism exists with its own peculiar tradition and development; in the Chamber in 1922 it numbered about twenty—out of the fifty-two deputies elected in the island.

We have said that the southern peasant is tied to the big property-owner through the activity of the intellectual. This tie-up is typical for the whole of the mainland South and Sicily. There has thus been created a monstrous agrarian *bloc* which as a whole acts as an inter-mediary and overseer for northern capital and the big banks. Its sole aim is to preserve the *status quo*. Inside it there is no intellectual light, no programme, no urge towards betterment and progress. If a few ideas and programmes have been put forward, they have had their origin outside the South, in the conservative agrarian political groups, especially in Tuscany, which were the parliamentary partners of the southern agrarian *bloc*. Sonnino and Franchetti were among the few intelligent bourgeois who saw the southern problem as a national problem and outlined a government plan for its solution. What was the point of view of Sonnino and Franchetti? The necessity of creating in southern Italy an independent middle stratum of such an economic character as would, as they then said, represent "public opinion", on the one hand limiting the arbitrary cruelties of the property-owners and on the other moderating the insurrectionism of the poor peasants. Sonnini and Franchetti were terrified by the popularity of the Bakuninist ideas of the First International in the South. This fear of theirs led them to make mistakes which were often grotesque. In one of their publications, for example, they mentioned that a popular inn in a Calabrian village (I am quoting from memory) was called "The Strikers" (*Scioperanti*) as proof of the insidious spread of the International's ideas. The fact, if it is a fact (as it must be if one accepts the writer's integrity) is more simply explicable if one recalls how numerous are the Albanian colonies in the South and how the word *Skipetari* has undergone many stranger and more curious alterations (thus in some documents of the Venetian Republic military formations of *S'ciopera* are spoken of). Now the trouble in the South was not so much that the theories of Bakunin were widespread, as that the situation itself was such as to have probably suggested his theories to Bakunin: certainly the poor southern peasants' thoughts turned to "ruination" long before Bakunin's brain had thought out the theory of "pandestruction".

The government plan of Sonnino and Franchetti never even got started, nor could it. The keystone of the relations between North and South in the organisation of the national economy and the State, is that the birth of a widespread middle class, in the economic sense (which means the birth of a widespread capitalist bourgeoisie), is rendered almost impossible. All accumulation of capital on the spot, and all accumulation of savings is rendered impossible by the fiscal and tariff system and by the fact that the capitalist owners of businesses do not transform their profit locally into new capital because they are not local people. When in the twentieth century emigration expanded on an enormous scale and the first returns began to flow from America, the liberal economists shouted triumphantly: Sonnino's dream will come true, a silent revolution is taking place in the South, which slowly but surely will change the whole economic and social structure of the country. But the State intervened and the silent revolution was suffocated at birth. The government offered treasury bonds at a certain interest and the emigrants and their families changed from being agents of the silent revolution into agents for giving the State the financial means for subsidising the parasitic industries of the North. Francesco Nitti who, as a democrat formally outside the southern agrarian *bloc* looked as if he were capable of realising Sonnino's programme, was in fact the best agent of northern capitalism for raking off the last resources of southern savings. The billions swallowed up by the *Banca di Sconto* came almost entirely from the South: the great majority of the 400,000 creditors were southern savers.

Above the agrarian *bloc* there functions in the South an intellectual *bloc* which in practice has up to now served to prevent the splits in the agrarian *bloc* becoming too dangerous and causing a landslide. The spokesmen of this intellectual *bloc* are Giustino Fortunato and Benedetto Croce, who for this reason can be regarded as the most industrious reactionaries of the peninsula.

We have said that Southern Italy is an area of extreme social disintegration. This formula can apply to the intellectuals as well as to the peasants. It is noteworthy that in the South, alongside the biggest properties, there have existed and do exist great accumulations of culture and intelligence in single individuals or in restricted groups of top intellectuals, whereas there exists no organisation of average culture. In the South there is the Laterza publishing house, and the review *La Critica*, there are the Academies and cultural enterprises of the greatest erudition; but there are no small and medium reviews, there are no publishing houses around which average groups of intellectuals gather. The southerners who have sought to leave the agrarian *bloc* and pose the southern question in a radical form have grouped themselves around reviews printed outside the South. Moreover it can be said that every cultural enterprise of the middle intellectuals launched in the twentieth century in central and northern Italy has been characterised by "southernism", since all have been strongly influenced by the southern intellectuals. So be it: the supreme political and intellectual moderators of all these enterprises have been Giustino Fortunato and Benedetto Croce. In far wider circles than the stifling circle of the agrarian *bloc* they have seen to it that the presentation of the southern problem should not exceed certain limits, should not become revolutionary. Being men of the greatest culture and intelligence, born out of the traditional soil of the South but tied to European and so to world culture, they have had enough talent to give some satisfaction to the intellectual needs of the more honest representatives of the cultured youth of the South, in order to assuage their restless, feeble longing for revolt against existing conditions, and to lead them into the middle way of classical serenity of thought and action. The so-called neo-Protestants or Calvinists have not understood that in Italy, since modern conditions of civilisation make any religious Reformation of the masses impossible, the only historically possible Reformation has taken place with the philosophy of Benedetto Croce: directions and methods of thought have been changed, a new conception of the world has been built up which has superseded Catholicism and every other mythological religion. In this sense Benedetto Croce has fulfilled a supreme "national" function: he has detached the radical intellectuals of the South from the peasant masses, making them share in national and European culture, and by means of this culture he has caused them to be absorbed by the national bourgeoisie and so by the agrarian *bloc*.

If in a certain sense *Ordine Nuovo* and the Turin Communists can be linked with the intellectual formations which we have mentioned, and if therefore they also have suffered the intellectual influence of Giustino Fortunato and Benedetto Croce, they nevertheless represent at the same time a complete break with that tradition and the beginning of a new development which has already yielded and will again yield fruits. As has already been said, they have made the urban proletariat the modern protagonist of Italian history and so of the southern question. Having served as intermediaries between the proletariat and

certain strata of left-wing intellectuals, they have succeeded in modifying, if not completely, certainly to a noteworthy extent, the latter's
mental orientation. This, if you think about it, is the principal element
in the figure of Piero Gobetti. He was not a Communist, and probably
would never have become one, but he understood the social and
historical position of the proletariat and his thought could no longer be
divorced from this element. Gobetti, in his newspaper work with us,
had been placed by us in contact with a living world which before he
had only known through books. His most outstanding characteristic was
his intellectual loyalty and complete absence of any vanity or pettiness:
because of this he could not but convince himself of the falsity of a
whole series of traditional ideas about the proletariat. What consequences did this contact with the proletarian world have for Gobetti?
It afforded the origin and impulse for a conception which we do not
wish to discuss and fathom here, a conception which in a great part
was linked up with syndicalism and the ways of thought of the
syndicalist intellectuals: the principles of liberalism were here raised
from the level of individual phenomena to that of mass phenomena.
The qualities of excess (*eccedenza*) and prestige in the life of individuals
are transferred into classes, conceived almost as collective individuals.
This conception usually leads the intellectuals who share it to pure
contemplation and awarding points, to the odious and stupid position
of arbiter between the contestants, of a bestower of prizes and punish-
ments. In practice Gobetti fled from this destiny. He showed himself
an organiser of culture of extraordinary value and he had in this last
period a function which must not be ignored or underestimated by the
workers. He dug a trench beyond which those more honest and
sincere groups of intellectuals who in 1919-20-21 felt that the proletariat would be superior as a ruling class to the bourgeoisie, did not
retreat. Some honestly and in good faith, others dishonestly and in
bad faith went around repeating that Gobetti was nothing but a
camouflaged Communist, an agent, if not of the Communist Party,
at least of the Communist group of *Ordine Nuovo*. It is not even
necessary to repudiate such silly tittle-tattle. The figure of Gobetti and
the movement represented by him were spontaneous products of the
new historical climate in Italy: in this lies their significance and importance. On some occasions there have been reproaches by Party

comrades for not having fought against this "liberal revolutionary" current of ideas; rather, this absence of a struggle seemed the proof of the organic link, of a Machiavellian character (as people used to say), between Gobetti and ourselves. We could not fight against Gobetti because he was developing and represented a movement which should not be fought, at least in principle. Not to understand this means not to understand the question of the intellectuals and the rôle which they play in the class struggle. In practice Gobetti served us as a link: (1) with the intellectuals born in the field of capitalist technique who had taken up a left-wing position, favourable to the dictatorship of the proletariat, in 1919-1920; (2) with a series of southern intellectuals, who as a result of more complex connections, saw the southern question on a different basis from the traditional one, introducing into it the proletariat of the North: of these intellectuals Guido Dorso is the most complete and interesting figure. Why ought we to have fought against the "Liberal Revolution" movement? Perhaps because it was not composed of pure Communists who had accepted our programme and doctrine from A to Z? This could not be demanded because it would have been politically and historically a paradox.

The intellectuals develop slowly, much more slowly than any other social group, because of their own nature and historical rôle. They represent the whole cultural tradition of a people, and they wish to recapitulate and synthetise the whole of [its] history: this may be said especially of the old type of intellectual, of the intellectual born on peasant soil. To think it possible that this type can, as a mass, break with the whole of the past in order to place itself wholeheartedly on the side of a new ideology, is absurd. It is absurd for the intellectuals as a mass, and perhaps absurd also for very many intellectuals taken individually, despite all the honest efforts they make and want to make. Now the intellectuals interest us as a mass, and not only as individuals. It is certainly important and useful for the proletariat that one or more intellectuals, individually, adhere to its programme and its doctrine, merge themselves with the proletariat, and become and feel themselves an integral part of it. The proletariat, as a class, is poor in organising elements, does not have and cannot form its own stratum of intellectuals except very slowly, very laboriously and only after the conquest of State power. But it is also important and useful that a break of an organic kind, characterised historically, is caused inside the mass of the intellectuals: that there is formed, as a mass formation, a left-wing tendency, in the modern sense of the word, that is, one which is orientated towards the revolutionary proletariat. The alliance between the proletariat and the peasant masses requires this formation: so much the more does the alliance between the proletariat and the peasant masses of the South require it. The proletariat will destroy the southern agrarian *bloc* to the extent to which, through its Party, it succeeds in organising ever larger masses of peasants in autonomous and independent formations; but it will succeed to a more or less large extent in this obligatory task according to its capacity to break up the intellectual *bloc* which forms the flexible but very resistant armour of the agrarian *bloc*. In carrying out this task the proletariat has been helped by Piero Gobetti and we believe that the friends of the dead man will continue even without his guidance the work which has been undertaken. This work is gigantic and difficult, but precisely because of this it is worthy of every sacrifice (even of life, as it has been in the case of Gobetti) on the part of those intellectuals of the North and the South (and they are many, more than one thinks), who have understood that only two social forces are essentially national and the bearers of the future: the proletariat and the peasants. . . . (Here the MS. is broken off.)

*Part Two*

*GRAMSCI IN PRISON, 1926–1937*

# INTRODUCTION

IN late November, 1926 the Fascist Government of Italy issued its "Exceptional laws for State security". By these all opposition parties were outlawed and their newspapers banned. The Fascist dictatorship had begun. Special tribunals were set up to try political suspects, outside the normal procedure of criminal law.

Gramsci was arrested in Rome on November 8th, 1926. At first he was exiled without trial to the island prison of Ustica, to the north of Sicily. After a few weeks he was transported back to Milan for trial. This was in January of 1927, but Gramsci had to wait for over a year for his trial. This finally took place in May, 1928, at Rome, where Gramsci was now transferred together with many other leading Italian Communists. The trial itself was a travesty. Gramsci was accused of plotting subversion of the State and fomenting class hatred and was finally sentenced to twenty years imprisonment. Just before sentence was passed the Public Prosecutor rose and pointed to Gramsci. "For twenty years", he demanded, "we must stop that brain from working."

There followed a nightmarish journey, through the heat of an exceptionally oppressive Italian summer, from Rome to the prison at Turi di Bari. The cattle truck in which Gramsci was chained so that he could neither lie down nor stand was allowed to wait for days on end in railways sidings. The whole journey lasted over a fortnight and took a terrible toll of Gramsci's always fragile health. He had been reported sick before leaving Rome but was denied medical attention. During the journey one side of his body broke out in painful boils and inflammations. By the time he reached Turi he was found to be in an almost complete state of physical collapse.

The years of Gramsci's imprisonment at Turi were a period of slow torture by which the already sick man was driven inexorably and cold-bloodedly to his death. Under the influence of an atrocious prison diet and non-existent medical care his health gradually broke down. With immense courage he sought to keep his personality intact, and his letters from prison are an intensely moving and inspiring document of the tenacity with which he strove to maintain his life and dignity. He was rarely able to eat more than a few spoonfuls of rice a day. Within a few years he had lost all his teeth and this further weakened his digestion. He suffered during his waking hours from acute intestinal pains.

These conditions were rendered immeasurably worse by the fact that every night during the first years of his imprisonment Gramsci was woken three times for "inspection". His cell was next to the guardroom and this further interfered with his sleep. In a letter dated November 3rd, 1930 Gramsci wrote: "I have worked out the statistics for October: I slept for five hours on only two nights, for nine nights I didn't sleep at all. Other nights I slept less than five hours. I myself am amazed that I still have so much resistance and have not yet had a general collapse."

Worst of all, perhaps, he suffered the mental torture of one who had always led a most active life, who rejoiced in the company of others, and who now found himself totally divorced from his friends, his fellow workers and his family. After his arrest he never saw his wife or two baby children again. His wife, Guilia Schucht, whom he had married in Moscow in 1923, returned to her native land and never recovered from the nervous shock of Gramsci's imprisonment. Yet throughout this period he never once doubted the correctness of the decision taken several years earlier to devote all his energies to the cause of socialism. To his sister he wrote: "My imprisonment is an episode in the political struggle which has been fought and will continue to be fought not only in Italy but in the whole world for who knows how long yet. I have been captured, just as during a war one could be taken prisoner, knowing that this and even worse could happen. . . ." But these words covered up an immense inner struggle to adjust his whole psychological and physical being to the conditions of prison life. He never engaged in self-pity and at the same time he refused to look upon himself as in any way a martyr. In his own words he was "eminently practical". "My practicality consists in this," he wrote to his sister-in-law, "in the knowledge that if you beat your head against the wall it is your head which breaks and not the wall . . . that is my strength, my only strength."

But Gramsci did in fact suffer two serious physical breakdowns—in May, 1931, and March, 1933, when he was thought to be on the point of death. The conditions of his imprisonment aroused the indignation of many leading intellectuals and others throughout free Europe, including Romain Rolland in France and the Archbishop of Canterbury.

In January, 1936, Gramsci was finally transferred from Turi to a clinic at Formia, and later, as his condition continued to deteriorate, to the Quisisana Clinic at Rome. But he was a dying man. His sentence was reduced by ten years but a week after his shortened sentence was up Gramsci died, on April 27th, 1937, after eleven years imprisonment.

The conditions of Gramsci's prison existence must be borne in mind when approaching the following selection from his prison writings. The writings themselves—2,848 closely packed pages in thirty-two notebooks—are themselves a testimony to his courage and determination. From early on he was tormented with the idea of not wasting his time and of using what freedom still remained to him to produce something "for posterity". He projected a broad scheme of work embracing the whole modern development of Italian society, especially in its cultural aspects. The subjects covered show the immense breadth of his interests and knowledge—Dante's *Inferno*, the dramatic significance of Pirandello (Gramsci was the first to acknowledge his rôle), Machiavelli, the struggle for national independence in the nineteenth century, popular superstition and folk-lore, the rôle of the Catholic Church, the development of the education system, modern journalism, modern industrial organisation, the philosophy of Benedetto Croce—these are a few of the essays and notes in the prison writings.

Gramsci wrote quickly, often not pausing to rewrite and often expressing himself elliptically in order to keep up with the torrent of ideas which poured out of his brain. He was writing notes and essays in the first instance for himself—he was not writing directly for publication. Often he would refer in passing to a book or an article and one is left uncertain as to the exact significance of the reference. Often sentence structure itself would be abandoned and the writings suddenly take the form of a series of jottings. There are many repetitions—ideas sketched out in an early writing taken up again and elaborated later.

The prison writings, therefore, do not make easy reading. They demand close attention and careful study. Each re-reading will be found to reveal fresh subtleties of thought which at first may be missed. These writings should not be looked on as essays or articles in the conventional sense, since many of them lack inner structure of the kind demanded by writings prepared for publication. In a sense each paragraph stands on its own, and the order of paragraphs is not always logical.

In order to avoid the ever-watchful eye of the prison supervision Gramsci was forced to use his own periphrasis when referring to controversial names or ideas. Thus he never mentioned Marxism but spoke instead of "the philosophy of action", and Marx and Engels are always referred to as "the founders of the philosophy of action." In this translation these circumlocutions have been dispensed with and the usual terms used for the sake of greater ease of reading.

# THE STUDY OF PHILOSOPHY AND OF
# HISTORICAL MATERIALISM

THE widespread prejudice that philosophy is something which is very difficult because it is the intellectual activity of a specific category of specialist scholars or of professional and systematic philosophers must be destroyed. To do this we must first show that all men are "philosophers", defining the limitations of this "spontaneous philosophy" possessed by "everyone", that is, of the philosophy which is contained in:

1. language itself, which is a totality of determined notions and concepts and not simply and solely of words grammatically void of content;

2. common sense and good sense;

3. popular religion and therefore also in the entire system of beliefs, superstitions, opinions, ways of perceiving and acting which make up what is generally called "folk-lore".

Having shown that everyone is a philosopher, even if in his own way, unconsciously (because even in the smallest manifestation of any intellectual activity—"language"—is contained a definite conception of the world), we pass to the second stage, the stage of criticism and awareness. We pass to the question: is it preferable to "think" without having critical awareness, in a disjointed and irregular way, in other words to "participate" in a conception of the world "imposed" mechanically by external environment, that is, by one of the many social groups in which everyone is automatically involved from the time he enters the conscious world (this might be one's own village or province, might have its origin in the parish and the "intellectual activity" of the curate or of the patriarchal old man whose "wisdom" is law, of the crone who has inherited the knowledge of the witches, or of the puny intellectual soured by his own stupidities and impotence); or is it preferable to work out one's own conception of the world consciously and critically, and so out of this work of one's own brain to choose one's own sphere of activity, to participate actively in making the history of the world, and not simply to accept passively and without care the imprint of one's own personality from outside?

Note 1. For his own conception of the world a man always belongs

to a certain grouping, and precisely to that of all the social elements
who share the same ways of thinking and working. He is a conformist
to some conformity, he is always man-mass or man-collective. The
question is this: of what historical type is the conformity, the man-mass,
of which he is a part? When his conception of the world is not critical
and coherent but haphazard and disconnected he belongs simultaneously to a multiplicity of men-masses, his own personality is made up
in a queer way. It contains elements of the cave-man and principles of
the most modern and advanced learning, shabby, local prejudices of all
past historical phases and intuitions of a future philosophy of the
human race united all over the world. Criticising one's own conception of the world means, therefore, to make it coherent and unified
and to raise it to the point reached by the most advanced modern
thought. It also means criticising all hitherto existing philosophy in
so far as it has left layers incorporated into the popular philosophy.
The beginning of the critical elaboration is the consciousness of what
one really is, that is, a "know thyself" as the product of the historical
process which has left you an infinity of traces gathered together
without the advantage of an inventory. First of all it is necessary to
compile such an inventory.

Note 2. Philosophy cannot be separated from the history of philosophy nor culture from the history of culture. In the most immediate and
pertinent sense one cannot be a philosopher, that is, have a critically
coherent conception of the world, without being aware of its history,
of the phases of development it represents and of the fact that it stands
in contradiction to other conceptions or elements of them. The correct
conception of the world answers certain problems posed by reality
which are very much determined and "original" in their actuality.
How is it possible to think about the present, and a very much determined present, with a thought elaborated from problems of a past
which is often remote and superseded? If this happens it means that
one is an "anachronism" in one's own time, a fossil and not a modern
living being. Or at least one is "made up" strangely. And in fact it
happens that social groups which in certain ways express the most
developed modernity, are retarded in others by their social position
and so are incapable of complete historical independence.

Note 3. If it is true that any language contains the elements of a conception of the world and of a culture, it will also be true that the greater or lesser complexity of a person's conception of the world can be judged from his language. A person who only speaks a dialect or who understands the national language in varying degrees necessarily enjoys a more or less restricted and provincial, fossilised and anachronistic perception of the world in comparison with the great currents of thought which dominate world history. His interests will be restricted, more or less corporative and economic, and not universal. If it is not always possible to learn foreign languages so as to put oneself in touch with different cultures, one must at least learn the national tongue. One great culture can be translated into the language of another great culture that is, one great national language which is historically rich and complex, can translate any other great culture, i.e. can be a world expression. But a dialect cannot do the same thing.

Note 4. The creation of a new culture does not only mean individually making some "original" discoveries. It means also and especially the critical propagation of truths already discovered, "socialising them" so to speak, and so making them become a basis for live action, an element of co-ordination and of intellectual and moral order. The leading of a mass of men to think coherently and in a unitary way about present-day reality is a "philosophical" fact of much greater importance and "originality" than the discovery by a philosophical "genius" of a new truth which remains the inheritance of small groups of intellectuals.

### Connection between Common Sense, Religion and Philosophy

Philosophy is an intellectual order such as neither religion nor common sense can be. See how, in reality, not even religion and common sense coincide, but religion is an element of disjointed common sense. For the rest, "common sense" is a collective noun like religion: there does not exist only one common sense, but this also is an historical product and development. Philosophy is criticism and the overcoming of religion and of common sense, and in this sense coincides with "good sense" which contrasts with common sense.

### Relationship between Science, Religion and Common Sense

Religion and common sense cannot constitute an intellectual order because they cannot be reduced to unity and coherence even in the individual consciousness: they cannot be reduced to unity and coherence "freely", though this could happen "authoritatively", as in fact has happened in the past within certain limits. The problem of religion is intended not in the confessional sense but in the lay sense of unity of faith between a conception of the world and a conforming norm of conduct: but why call this unity of faith "religion" and not call it "ideology", or actually "politics"?

Philosophy in general does not in fact exist: various philosophies and conceptions of the world exist and one always makes a choice between them. How does this choice come about? Is it merely intellectual or is it more complex? And does it not often happen that there is a contradiction between the intellectual fact and the norm of conduct? What then will the real conception of the world be: the one which is logically affirmed as an intellectual fact or the one which results from the real activity of a certain person, which is implicit in his actions? And since actions are always political actions, can we not say that the real philosophy of anyone is contained in his politics? This conflict between thought and action, that is, the co-existence of two conceptions of the world, one affirmed in words and the other explaining itself in effective actions, is not always due to bad faith. Bad faith can be a satisfactory explanation for some individuals taken singly, or even for more or less numerous groups, but it is not satisfactory when the contrast shows itself in the life of large masses: then it cannot be other than the expression of more profound contradictions of an historical and social order. It means that a social group, which has its own conception of the world, even through embryonic (which shows itself in actions, and so only spasmodically, occasionally, that is, when such a group moves as an organic unity) has, as a result of intellectual subordination and submission, borrowed a conception which is not its own from another group, and this it affirms in words. And this borrowed conception also it believes it is following, because it follows it in "normal" times, when its conduct is not independent and autonomous but precisely subordinate and submissive. That is why we cannot separate philosophy from politics. On the contrary, we can show that the choice and criticism of a conception of the world is itself a political fact.

So we must explain how it comes about that in every period there coexist many philosophical systems and trends, how they originate and how they are propagated, because in their propagation they divide and follow certain directions, etc. This shows how necessary it is to systematise one's own intuitions of the world and of life critically and coherently, fixing exactly what must be meant by "system", because it should not be understood in the pedantic and academic sense of the word. But this elaboration must be and can only be made within the framework of a history of philosophy which shows what elaboration thought has undergone in the course of the centuries, what collective effort it has cost to arrive at our present mode of thinking which recapitulates and summarises all this past history, including its errors and delusions—which, however, does not mean that, because they have been trusted in the past and have been corrected, they should be reproduced in the present and are still correct.

What idea does the people have of philosophy? We can build this up from popular phrases. One of the most widespread is that of "looking at things philosophically", which if we analyse it, is not to be entirely rejected. It is true that it contains an implicit invitation to resignation and patience, but it seems really that the more important point is the invitation to reflection, to explain to oneself that what is happening is at bottom rational and that it should be faced up to as such, concentrating one's own rational powers and not letting oneself be dragged along by instinctive and violent impulses. These popular sayings could be collected together with the similar expressions of popular writers—taking them from the large dictionaries—where we find the terms "philosophy" and "philosophically", and we would see that these words have a very precise significance—overcoming animal and elemental passions with a conception of necessity which gives to one's own actions a conscious direction. This is the sound nucleus of common sense. It can certainly be called good sense and deserves to be developed and rendered unitary and coherent. So it appears that for this reason also it is not possible to distinguish what is called "learned" philosophy from "vulgar" popular philosophy which is only a disjointed complex of ideas and opinions.

But at this point we pose the fundamental problem of every conception of the world view, of every philosophy which has become a cultural movement, a "religion", a "faith", in other words, which has led to practical activity and volition, in which it appears as an implied theoretical "premise". (It could be called an "ideology" if this is given the higher meaning of a world view showing itself implicitly in art, law, economic activity and in all the manifestations of individual and collective life.) It is the problem of conserving the ideological unity of a whole social *bloc* which is held together and unified precisely by that ideology. The power of religions and especially of the Catholic Church has consisted and does consist in the fact that they feel strongly the need for the doctrinal unity of the whole "religious" mass, and struggle to prevent the superior intellectual elements detaching themselves from the inferior ones. The Roman church has always been the most tenacious in the struggle to avoid the "official" formation of two religions, one for the "intellectuals" and one for the "simple people". This struggle has not always been fought without serious inconvenience for the church itself, but this inconvenience is connected with the historical process which transforms the whole of civil society and which *en bloc* contains a criticism destructive of religions; so much the greater has been the organising capacity of the clergy in the sphere of culture and the abstractly rational and correct relationship which in its own circle it has been able to establish between the intellectuals and the simple folk. The greatest architects of this equilibrium have undoubtedly been the Jesuits, and to conserve it they have imprinted on the Church a progressive movement which aims to give a certain satisfaction to the requirements of science and philosophy, but with such a slow and methodical rhythm that the changes are not seen by the mass of the simple people, even though they appear "revolutionary" and demagogical to the "integralists".

One of the major weaknesses of the immanentist philosophies in general consists precisely in their not having been able to create an ideological unity between the lower and the upper, between the "simple people" and the intellectuals. In the history of western civilisation this was proved on a European scale by the failure of the Renaissance and partly also of the Reformation in the face of the Roman church. This weakness appears in the schools inasmuch as the immanentist philosophies have not even tried to build up a conception which could be substituted for religion in child education. Hence the pseudo-historical sophism by which non-religious (non-confessional) teachers who are really atheists allow the teaching of religion, because religion is the philosophy of mankind's infancy which is renewed in every un-metaphorical infancy. Idealism has also shown itself opposed to cultural movements of "going to the people", such as the so-called People's Universities and similar bodies, and not only because they were deteriorating, for in such a case it should have only sought to improve them. However, these movements were worth attention and deserved to be studied. They could have prospered, inasmuch as they showed a sincere enthusiasm and a strong will on the part of the "simple people" to raise themselves to a higher form of culture and world view. But they lacked any organism whether of philosophic thought or of organised strength and cultural centralisation. One had the impression that they resembled the first contacts between English merchants and the Negroes of Africa; they gave second-rate goods in return for gold nuggets. On the other hand, organism of thought and cultural solidarity could only have been brought about if there had existed between the intellectuals and the simple people that unity which there should have been between theory and practice; if, that is, the intellectuals had been organically the intellectuals of those masses, if they had elaborated and made coherent the principles and problems which those masses posed by their practical activity, in this way constituting a cultural and social *bloc*. It comes back to the question we have already emphasised: is it sufficient for a philosophical movement to devote itself to the development of a specialised culture for restricted groups of intellectuals, or must it, in elaborating a thought which is superior to common sense and scientifically coherent, never forget to remain in contact with the "simple people" and, moreover, find in this contact the source of its problems to be studied and solved? Only through this contact does a philosophy become "historic", does it cleanse itself of intellectualist elements of an individual nature and make itself into "life".[1]

[1] Perhaps it is useful "in practice" to distinguish between philosophy and common sense in order better to show the transition from one stage to the other; in philosophy the characteristics of the individual elaboration of a thought are especially prominent; in common sense, however, it is the confused and dispersed characteristics of a generic thought of a certain epoch and a certain popular environment. But every philosophy tends to become common sense also within a restricted environment (of all the intellectuals). The point is one of elaborating a philosophy which has already been or is capable of being propagated, because it is linked with practical life and implicit in it, and which may become a new common sense with the same coherence and force as the individual philosophies. This cannot happen unless the need is continually felt for cultural contact with the "simple people".

Marxism can only present itself at first in a style of polemic and criticism, as overcoming preceding modes of thought and actual existing thought (or the existing cultural world); hence above all as a critique of "common sense" (after having based itself on common sense to demonstrate that "everyone" is a philosopher and that it is not a question of introducing *ex novo* a science into the individual life of "everyone", but of renovating and criticising an already existing philosophy) and hence also as a critique of the philosophies of the intellectuals which make up the history of philosophy, and which, individually (and developing in fact essentially out of the activity of especially gifted individuals) can be considered as the "high points" of the progress of common sense, at least of the common sense of the more cultured strata of society, and through them of popular common sense as well. That is why an introduction to the study of philosophy must expound synthetically the problems nascent in the development of general culture, which is only partially reflected in the history of philosophy, the latter, however, in the absence of a history of common sense (impossible to write because of the lack of documentary material) remaining the largest source of reference—in order to discuss them, showing their living significance (if they still have any) or their significance in the past as links in a historical chain, and determining the new present-day problems or the present-day formulation of old problems.

The relationship between the "higher" philosophy and common sense is secured by "politics", just as the relationship between the Catholicism of the intellectuals and that of the "simple people" is secured by politics. But the difference in the two cases is fundamental. The fact that the Church has to face the problem of the "simple people" means precisely that a breach has occurred within the community of the "faithful", a breach which cannot be healed by bringing the "simple people" up to the level of the intellectuals (the Church does not even set itself this task, which is ideally and economically too great for its actual forces), but by an iron discipline over the intellectuals so that they do not pass beyond certain limits of differentiation and do not render it catastrophic and irreparable. In the past these "breaches" in the community of the faithful were healed by strong mass movements which brought about, or were absorbed by, the formation of new religious orders around forceful personalities (Francis, Dominic).[1]

But the counter-Reformation sterilised this germination of popular forces. The Society of Jesus is the last great religious order, of reactionary and authoritarian origin, with a repressive and "diplomatic" character, whose origin signalised a stiffening of the Catholic organism. The new orders which arose afterwards had very small "religious" significance but great "disciplinary" significance over the masses of the faithful. They are ramifications and tentacles of the Society of Jesus or they have become such—weapons of "resistance" for preserving the already acquired political position, not forces of renewed development. Catholicism has become "Jesuitism". The modern age has not seen the creation of "religious orders" but of a political party, the Christian Democrats.[2]

Marxism is antithetical to this Catholic position: Marxism does not seek to sustain the "simple people" in their primitive philosophy of common sense, but instead to lead them to a higher view of life. If it asserts the need for contact between the intellectuals and the simple people it does so, not in order to limit scientific activity and maintain unity at the low level of the masses, but precisely in order to build an intellectual-moral *bloc* which makes politically possible the intellectual progress of the masses and not only of a few groups of intellectuals.

The active man of the masses works practically, but he does not have a clear theoretical consciousness of his actions, which is also a knowledge of the world in so far as he changes it. Rather his theoretical consciousness may be historically opposed to his actions. We can almost say that he has two theoretical consciousnesses (or one contradictory consciousness), one implicit in his actions, which unites him with all his colleagues in the practical transformation of reality, and one superficially explicit or verbal which he has inherited from the past and which he accepts without criticism. Nevertheless, this (superficial)

[1] The heretical movements of the middle ages, as simultaneous reactions to the political interference of the Church and to the scholastic philosophy of which it was an expression, on the basis of social conflicts determined by the rise of the communes, were a breach between the masses and the intellectuals inside the Church, which was healed by the rise of the popular religious movements absorbed by the Church in the formation of the mendicant orders and in a new religious unity.

[2] Remember the anecdote told by Steed in his *Memoires of the Cardinal* who explains to the philo-Catholic English Protestant that the miracles of St. Gennaro are articles of faith for the Neapolitan populace but not for the intellectuals, and that there are some "exaggerations" even in the Gospels. To the question: "Are we not Christians?" he replies: "We are 'prelates', that is, 'politicians' of the Church of Rome."

"verbal" conception is not without consequence; it binds him to a certain social group, influences his moral behaviour and the direction of his will in a more or less powerful way, and it can reach the point where the contradiction of his conscience will not permit any action, any decision, any choice, and produces a state of moral and political passivity. Critical understanding of oneself, therefore, comes through the struggle of political "hegemonies", of opposing directions, first in the field of ethics, then of politics, culminating in a higher elaboration of one's own conception of reality. The awareness of being part of a determined hegemonic force (i.e. political consciousness) is the first step towards a further and progressive self-consciousness in which theory and practice finally unite. So the unity of theory and practice is also not a given mechanical fact but an historical process of becoming, which has its elementary and primitive phases in the sense of "distinctiveness", of "separation", of barely instinctive independence, and progresses up to the real and complete possession of a coherent and unitary conception of the world. That is why we should emphasise that the political development of the concept of hegemony represents a great step forward in philosophy as well as in practical politics, because it involves and presupposes an intellectual unity and an ethic conforming to a conception of reality which has surpassed common sense and, even though still within restricted limits, has become critical.

However, in the most recent developments of Marxism the deepening of the concept of the unity of theory and practice is still only in its initial stage: remnants of mechanicalism still persist, since theory is spoken of as a "complement", an accessory of practice, as an ancillary of practice. It seems correct that this question, too, must be posed historically, that is, as an aspect of the political question of the intellectuals. Critical self-consciousness signifies historically and politically the creation of intellectual cadres: a human mass does not "distinguish" itself and does not become independent "by itself", without organising itself (in a broad sense) and there is no organisation without intellectuals, that is, without organisers and leaders, without the theoretical aspect of the theory-practice nexus distinguishing itself concretely in a stratum of people who "specialise" in its conceptual and philosophical elaboration. But this process of the creation of intellectuals is a long and difficult one, full of contradictions, of advances and retreats, of disbandings and regroupings, in which the "fidelity" of the mass ("fidelity" and discipline are initially the forms assumed by the adherence of the mass and by its collaboration in the development of the whole cultural phenomenon) is sometimes put to a severe test. The process of development is bound by an intellectuals-mass dialectic; the stratum of intellectuals develops quantitatively and qualitatively, but every leap towards a new "fullness" and complexity on the part of the intellectuals is tied to an analogous movement of the mass of simple people, who raise themselves to higher levels of culture and at the same time broaden their circle of influence with thrusts forward by more or less important individuals or groups towards the level of the specialised intellectuals. But in the process, times continually occur when a separation takes place between the mass and the intellectuals (either certain individuals or a group of them), a loss of contact, and hence the impression [of theory] as a complementary, subordinate "accessory". Insistence on the element of "practice" in the theory-practice nexus, after having split, separated and not merely distinguished the two elements (merely a mechanical and conventiona operation), means that we are passing through a relatively primitive historical phase, one that is still economic-corporative, in which the general framework of the "structure" is being transformed quantitatively and the appropriate quality-superstructure is in process of arising but is not yet organically formed. We must emphasise the importance and significance which the political parties have in the modern world in the elaboration and propagation of conceptions of the world, inasmuch as they elaborate an ethic and a policy suited to themselves, that is, they act almost as historical "experimenters" with these conceptions. Parties individually select a working mass and this selection takes place in the practical as well as the theoretical fields, with a stricter relationship between theory and practice according as their conceptions are more vitally and radically innovatory and antagonistic to the old modes of thought. Hence one can say that the parties are the elaborators of new integrated and all-embracing intellectual systems, in other words the annealing agents of the unity of theory and practice in the sense of real historical process. Of course, it is necessary that the parties should be formed through individual enlistment and not in a "Labour Party" way (i.e. by affiliated members, *Trans.*), because, if

the aim is to lead organically "the whole economically active mass"
it must be led not according to old schemes but by creating new ones,
and the innovation cannot involve the mass, in its first stages, except
by way of a *cadre* in whom the conception implicit in the human
activity has already become to a certain extent actually coherent and
systematic consciousness, precise and decided will.

One of these phases can be studied in the discussion through which
the most recent developments of Marxism have been asserted, a
discussion summarised in an article by D. S. Mirsky, an associate of
the review *Cultura*. We can see how the transition took place from a
mechanistic and purely external conception to an activist conception,
which, as has been observed, approached more nearly a correct
understanding of the unity of theory and practice, although it has not
yet reached its full synthetic significance. We can observe how the
determinist, fatalist mechanist element has been an immediate ideological "aroma" of Marxism, a form of religion and of stimulation
(but like a drug necessitated and historically justified by the "subordinate" character of certain social strata).

When one does not have the initiative in the struggle and the struggle
itself is ultimately identified with a series of defeats, mechanical
determinism becomes a formidable power of moral resistance, of
patient and obstinate perseverance. "I am defeated for the moment
but the nature of things is on my side over a long period," etc. Real
will is disguised as an act of faith, a sure rationality of history, a
primitive and empirical form of impassioned finalism which appears
as a substitute for the predestination, providence, etc., of the confessional religions. We must insist on the fact that even in such cases
there exists in reality a strong active will, a direct influence on the
"nature of things", but it is certainly in an implicit and veiled form,
ashamed of itself, and so the consciousness of it is contradictory, lacks
critical unity, etc. But when the "subordinate" becomes the leader
and is responsible for the economic activity of the mass, mechanicalism
appears at a certain moment as an imminent danger, there occurs a
revision of the whole mode of thinking because there has taken place
a change in the social mode of being. Why do the limits of the power
of the "nature of things" come to be restricted? Because, at bottom,
if the subordinate was yesterday a thing, today he is no longer a thing

but an historical person, a protagonist; if yesterday he was irresponsible because he was "resisting" an outside will, today he feels responsible because he is no longer resisting but is an agent and so necessarily active and enterprising. But even yesterday had he ever been mere "thing", mere "irresponsibility"? Surely not. Rather we should stress how fatalism has only been a cover by the weak for an active and real will. This is why it is always necessary to show the futility of mechanical determinism, which, explicable as a naïve philosophy of the masses, and only as such as an intrinsic element of power, becomes a cause of passivity, of imbecilic self-sufficiency, when it is made into a reflexive and coherent philosophy on the part of the intellectuals, and this without expecting that the subordinate may become leading and responsible. One part even of the subordinate mass is always leading and responsible and the philosophy of the part precedes the philosophy of the whole, not only as theoretical anticipation but as actual necessity.

That the mechanist conception has been the religion of subordinates appears from an analysis of the development of the Christian religion. In certain periods and under given historical conditions this has been and continues to be a "necessity", a necessary form assumed by the will of the masses, a determined form of rationality of the world and of life, and has supplied the *cadres* for real practical activity. In this little extract from an article in *Civilta Cattolica* (March 5th, 1932), this rôle of Christianity seems to me to be well expressed: "Faith in a secure future, in the immortality of the soul destined to bliss, in the security of being able to reach eternal joy, was the main-spring for a work of intense internal perfection and of spiritual elevation. True Christian individualism has found in this the incentive for its victories. All the powers of the Christian were concentrated around this noble end. Freed from speculative fluctuations which wore down the soul with doubt, and enlightened by immortal principles, man felt his hopes reborn; sure that a higher power sustained him in the struggle against evil, he did violence to himself and conquered the world." But even in this case what is meant is naïve Christianity; not Jesuitised Christianity, which has become simply opium for the people.

The position of Calvinism, with its iron conception of predestination and grace, which caused a vast expansion of the spirit of enterprise (or became the form of this movement), is still more expressive and significant.

In the course of becoming popular, why and how are new conceptions of the world propagated? In this process of propagation (which is at the same time a substitution for the old, and very often a combination between old and new) is there any influence exerted (how and to what extent) by the rational form in which the new conception is expounded and presented, the authority of the expounder (in so far as he is recognised and valued at least generally) and by the thinkers and scholars whom the expounder calls to his aid, and by membership of the same organisation as those who support the new conception (but only after having entered the organisation for other motives than that of sharing in the new conception)? These elements in fact vary according to the social group and the level of culture of that group. But research is especially interesting with regard to the masses who change their ideas with greater difficulty, and who never change them, in any case, by accepting the new ideas in their "pure" form, so to speak, but always only in more or less strange and weird combinations. The rational, logically coherent form, the completeness of the reasoning which neglects no positive or negative argument of any weight, has its importance, but it is a very long way from being decisive; it can be decisive in a minor way, when a given person is already in a state of intellectual crisis, drifts between the old and the new, has lost faith in the old but is not yet decided in favour of the new, etc.

So much can be said for the influence of the thinkers and scholars. It is very great among the people, but in fact every conception has its own thinkers and scholars, and so their authority is divided; and further, any thinker may analyse and cast doubt on what he himself has said, etc. We can conclude that the process of propagation of new conceptions takes place for political, that is, in the last instance, social reasons, but that the formal elements of logical coherence, authority and of organisation have a very great rôle in this process immediately after the general orientation has taken place, among individuals as well as large groups. From this we conclude that among the masses as such, philosophy can only exist as a faith. Besides, one may well imagine the intellectual position of a man of the people; he is made up of opinions, convictions, criteria of discrimination and norms of conduct. Anyone who supports a point of view contrary to his is able, in so far as he is intellectually superior, to argue better than him and put him logically to flight, etc.; should the man of the people therefore change his convictions? Because in the immediate discussion he is unable to assert himself? But then he would reach the position of having to change his ideas once a day, or every time he meets an ideological opponent who is intellectually superior to him. On what elements then is his philosophy based, and especially his philosophy in the form in which it has greater importance for him as a norm of conduct? The most important element is undoubtedly of a non-rational character, of faith. But in whom and in what? Especially in the social group to which he belongs, in so far as it thinks broadly as he does; the man of the people thinks that on such a basic thing so many cannot be so completely mistaken as his opponent in argument would like to make him believe; that he himself, it is true, is unable to support and develop his arguments as well as his opponent does his, but that in his own group there are people who are able to do so, in fact even better than this particular opponent. He remembers having heard the reasons for his faith expounded fully, coherently and in such a way that he remained convinced by them. He does not remember the actual arguments and could not repeat them. The fact that he was once convinced, as if by a clap of thunder, is the permanent reason for the persistence of the conviction, even if he is no longer able to argue for it.

But these considerations lead to the conclusion that the masses are extremely unreliable about new convictions, especially if these convictions are opposed to the (also new) orthodox convictions, which conform socially with the general interests of the ruling classes. One can see this reflected in the fortunes of religions and churches. A religion or a certain church maintains its own community of faithful people (within certain limits of the necessity of general historical development) to the extent to which it keeps alive its faith in a permanent and organised way, tirelessly repeating the apologetics, battling at all times and always with similar arguments and maintaining a hierarchy of intellectuals who give the faith at least the appearance of dignity of thought. Every time that the continuity of contact between the Church and the faithful has been violently broken for political reasons, as happened during the French Revolution, the loss suffered by the Church has been incalculable, and, if the conditions in which it was difficult to exercise the habitual practices had been prolonged beyond certain limits, it is conceivable that these losses would have proved decisive and a new religion would have arisen, in the same way as in fact in France it arose in combination with the former Catholicism. Certain essentials are deducible from this for every cultural movement which aims to replace common sense and the former conceptions of the world in general: (1) never tire of repeating its arguments (changing the literal form): repetition is the most effective didactic means of influencing the popular mind. (2) Work incessantly to raise the intellectual level of ever-widening strata of the people, that is, by giving personality to the amorphous element of the masses, which means working to produce *cadres* of intellectuals of a new type who arise directly from the masses though remaining in contact with them and becoming "the stay of the corset". This second necessity, if satisfied, is the one which really changes the "ideological panorama" of an age. On the other hand, these *cadres* cannot be constituted and develop without there appearing among them a hierarchy of authority and of intellectual competence, which may culminate in one great individual philosopher, if he is capable of re-living concretely the needs of the ideological community of the masses, of understanding that the mass cannot have the quickness and agility of an individual brain, and so succeeds in formally elaborating the collective doctrine in a way which is most akin and appropriate to the modes of thought of a collective thinker.

It is evident that a mass build-up of this kind cannot happen "arbitrarily" around any ideology, through the formally constructive will of one personality or of a group which proposes it out of fanaticism for its own philosophical or religious convictions. The consent or dissent of the masses for an ideology is the means by which real criticism of the rationality or historicity of modes of thought makes itself apparent. Arbitrary developments are more or less rapidly eliminated by historical competition, even if sometimes, through a favourable combination of immediate circumstances, they succeed in enjoying a certain popularity, while developments which correspond to the needs of a complex and organic historical age always end by gaining the upper hand and prevailing, even if they pass through many intermediary phases in which they asserted themselves in more or less strange and weird combinations.

These developments pose many problems, the most important of

which come under the heading of the kind and quality of the relationship between the variously qualified intellectual strata, that is, of the
importance of the rôle which the creative contributions of the upper
groups ought and are able to play in relation to the organic capacity for
discussion and development of new critical concepts on the part of
the intellectually subordinate strata. The point, therefore, is to fix the
limits for the freedom of discussion and propaganda, freedom which
must not be understood in the administrative or police sense but in
the sense of self-imposed limits which the leaders place on their own
activity or, properly speaking, of determining the direction of cultural
policy. In other words: who will decide the "laws of scholarship" and
the limits of scientific research, and can these laws and limits be properly
fixed? It seems necessary that the hard work of research for new truths
and for better, more coherent and clear formulation of the truths
themselves should be left to the free initiative of individual scholars,
even if they continually replace in discussion the very principles which
appear most essential. Besides, it will not be difficult to make clear
when such discussions have interested motives and are not of a scientific
character. It is not impossible to suggest that individual ideas might
be disciplined and ordered by passing them through the sieve of
academies and cultural institutions of various kinds, and that only
after they had been selected should they become public, etc.

It would be interesting to study concretely, for each country, the
cultural organisation which keeps the ideological world in movement,
and to examine its practical functioning. A study of the numerical
relations between the personnel which is professionally devoted to
active cultural work and the population of the various countries would
also be useful, together with an approximate calculation of the free
forces. The school, in all its levels, and the church are the two major
cultural organisations in every country, if one takes into account the
number of people they employ. In addition there are newspapers,
reviews and books, private scholastic institutions, whether linked with
the State school or as cultural institutions like the Popular Universities.
Other professions incorporate into their specialised activities a not
unimportant cultural section, such as that of the doctors, the army
officers, the lawyers. But it should be noted that in all countries, even
though to different extents, there exists a great breach between the

masses of the people and the groups of intellectuals, even the more numerous and nearest to the periphery of the nation, such as the school-masters and the priests. And this happens because, even where the rulers assert it in words, the State as such has no unitary, coherent and homogeneous conception. Because of this the intellectuals are separated into different strata, and again separated within each stratum. The university, except in some countries, does not exercise any unifying influence: often a free thinker has more influence than all the university institutions, etc.

With regard to the historical rôle played by the fatalist interpretation of Marxism, one could pronounce a funeral eulogy of it, vindicating its usefulness for a certain historical period but precisely because of this urging the necessity of burying it with all honours. Its rôle could be likened to that of the theory of grace and predestination for the beginnings of the modern world, which, however, culminated in the classical German philosophy with its conception of freedom as the awareness of necessity. It has been a popular substitute of the cry "God wills it", although even on this primitive and elementary plane it was the beginning of a more modern and fertile conception than that contained in the cry "God wills it" or in the theory of grace. Is it possible that "formally" a new conception should present itself in other garb than the rough unadorned dress of the plebian? Nevertheless the historian, with all the necessary perspective, succeeds in establishing and understanding that the beginnings of a new world, always hard and stony, are superior to the agonies of a declining world and to the swan-song which it brings forth.

# WHAT IS MAN?

THIS is the primary and main question in philosophy. How can it be answered? The definition is to be found in man himself, and therefore in each single man. But is this correct? In each single man, we will discover what each "single man" is. But we are not interested in what each single man is, which, after all, signifies what each single man is at each single moment. When we consider it, we find that by putting the question "What is man?" we really mean; "What can man become?", that is, whether or not man can control his own destiny, can "make himself", can create a life for himself. Therefore we say that man is a process, and precisely the process of his actions. When we consider it, the question "What is man?" is not an abstract or "objective" question. It stems from what we have thought about ourselves and others, and, relative to what we have thought and seen, we seek to know what we are and what we can become, whether it is true and within what limits that we do "make ourselves", create our own lives and our own destinies. We want to know this "now", in the given conditions of the present and of our "daily" life, and not about any life and about any man.

The question arises and derives its content from special, or rather, determined patterns of considering the life of man; the most important of these patterns is the "religious" one and a given religious one—Catholicism. Actually when we ask ourselves "what is man, how important is his will and his concrete activity in the creation of himself and the life he lives?" what we mean is: "Is Catholicism a true concept of man and of life? In being a Catholic, in making Catholicism a way of life, are we mistaken or right?" Everyone has the vague intuition that to make Catholicism a way of life is a mistake, because no one completely embraces Catholicism as a way of life even while declaring himself a Catholic. A strict Catholic who applied Catholic rules to every act of his life would appear as a monster; and this, when one thinks about it, is the strongest, most irrefutable criticism of Catholicism itself.

Catholics will reply by saying that no concepts are rigidly followed, and they are right. But this only proves that there does not in fact exist historically one rule and no other for thinking and functioning that applies equally to all men. It is no argument for Catholicism, even though this way of thinking and acting has for centuries been organised to this end—something which has not yet happened with any other religion with the same means at its disposal, the same spirit of system, the same continuity and centralisation. From the "philosophical" point of view, Catholicism's failure to satisfy rests in the fact that despite everything, it roots the cause of all evil in man himself, that is, it conceives of man as a clearly defined and limited individual. It can be said that all philosophies up to the present repeat this position taken by the Catholics; man is conceived of as limited by his individuality, and his spirit as well. It is precisely on this point that a change in the conception of man is required. That is, it is essential to conceive of man as a series of active relationships (a process) in which individuality, while of the greatest importance, is not the sole element to be considered. The humanity reflected in every individual consists of various elements: (1) the individual, (2) other men, (3) nature. The second and third elements are not as simple as they seem. The individual does not enter into relations with other men in opposition to them but through an organic unity with them, because he becomes part of social organisms of all kinds from the simplest to the most complex. Thus man does not enter into relationship with nature simply because he is himself part of nature, but actively, through work and through techniques. More. These relationships are not mechanical. They are active and conscious, and they correspond to the lesser or greater intelligence which the individual man possesses; therefore one can say that man changes himself, modifies himself, to the same extent that he changes and modifies the whole complex of relationships of which he is the nexus. In this sense the true philosopher is, and cannot avoid being political—that is, man active, who changes his environment—environment being understood to include the relationships into which each individual enters. If individuality is the whole mass of these relationships, the acquiring of a personality means the acquiring of consciousness of these relationships, and changing the personality means changing the whole mass of these relationships.

But, as stated earlier, these relationships are not simple. Moreover, some are involuntary and some voluntary. Furthermore, the very fact of being more or less profoundly conscious (knowing more or less of the way in which these relationships can be modified) already modifies them. Once recognised as necessary, these same necessary relationships change in aspect and importance. In this sense, recognition is power. But this problem is complicated in still another aspect; it is not enough to know the totality of the relations as they exist in a given moment within a given pattern; it is important to know their genesis, the impulse of their formation, because each individual is not only the synthesis of existing relations but also the history of these relations, the sum of all of the past. It will be said that what each individual is able to change is very little indeed. But considering that each individual is able to associate himself with all others who desire the same changes as himself, and provided the change is a rational one, the single individual is able to multiply himself by an impressive number and can thus obtain a far more radical change than would first appear.

The number of societies in which an individual can participate are very great (more than one thinks). It is through these "societies" that the individual plays a part in the human species. Thus the ways in which the individual enters into relations with nature are multiple, because by techniques we mean not only the totality of scientific ideas applied to industry in the usual meaning of the word, but also "mental" instruments, philosophic knowledge.

It is a commonplace that it is impossible to conceive of man otherwise than as existing in a society, but not all the necessary conclusions, even those applying to individuals, are always drawn. It is also a commonplace that for a given society there must be a given society of things, and that human society is only possible in so far as there exists a given society of things. These organisms apart from individual cases, have up to now been given a mechanist and determinist significance (both *societas hominum* and *societas rerum*); hence the reaction. It is essential to evolve a theory in which all these relationships are seen as active and in motion, establishing clearly that the source of this activity is man's individual consciousness which knows, wills, strives, creates because he already knows, desires, strives, creates, etc., and conceives of himself not as an isolated individual but rich in the potentialities offered by other men and by the society of things of which he must have some knowledge (because each man is a philosopher, a scientist, etc.).

Feuerbach's thesis: "Man is what he eats", if taken by itself, can be interpreted in various ways. Interpreted narrowly and foolishly, one could say: "Man is alternately what he eats materially", or—foods have an immediate determining influence on modes of thinking. It calls to mind Amadea Mordiga's statement, for instance, that if one knew what a man had eaten before he made a speech one could better interpret the speech itself—a childish statement and actually one that is alien even to positive science, because the brain is not nourished by beans and truffles but by foods which are transformed into homogeneous assimilable material and which unite to form the cells of the brain; that is, foods have potentially a "similar nature" to cerebral cells. If this statement were true, the matrix of history would be found in the kitchen, and revolutions would coincide with radical changes in the diet of the masses. Historical truth proves the contrary. It is revolutionary and complex historical development which has changed feeding habits and created successive "tastes" in the selection of food. It was not the regular sowing of grain which brought nomadism to a halt but vice versa, it was the conditions developing out of nomad life which forced regular cultivation, etc.

However, since diet is one expression of complex social relationships and each social regrouping has a basic food pattern, there is some truth in the saying "man is what he eats", but in the same way one could say "man is the clothing he wears", man is his habitation, man is his particular way of reproducing himself, or "he is his family", because food, dress, housing, and reproducing are elements of social life in which, in point of fact, the whole complex of social relations are most obviously and most widely manifested.

Thus the problem of what man is is always posed as the problem of so-called "human nature", or of "man in general", the attempt to create a science of man (a philosophy) whose point of departure is primarily based on a "unitary" idea, on an abstraction designed to contain all that is "human". But is "humanity", as a reality and as an idea, a point of departure—or a point of arrival? Or isn't it rather that

when posed as a point of departure, the attempt is reduced to a sur-
vival of theology and metaphysics? Philosophy cannot be reduced to
naturalistic anthropology; unity in mankind is not a quality of man's
biological nature; the differences in man which matter in history are
not the biological differences (of race, skull formation, skin colour,
etc.), from which is deduced the theory that man is what he eats. In
Europe man eats grain, in Asia, rice, etc.—which can then be reduced
to the other statement: "Man is the country he inhabits", because diet
is generally related to the country inhabited. And not even "biological
unity" has counted for much in history (man is the animal who
devoured his own kind when he was closest to the "natural state",
before he was able "artificially" to multiply production of natural
benefits). Nor did the "faculty of reasoning" or "spirit" create unity;
it cannot be recognised as a "unifying" fact because it is a categorical
formal concept. It is not "thought" but what is actually thought which
unites and differentiates men.

The most satisfying answer is that "human nature" is a "complex of
human relations", because this answer includes the idea of "becoming"
(man becomes, changes himself continually with the changing of social
relations), and because it denies "man in general". In reality social
relations are expressed by diverse groups of men which are presupposed
and the unity of which is dialectical and not formal. Man is aristocratic because he is the servant of the soil, etc. It can also be
said that man's nature is "history" (and in this sense, history equals
spirit, the nature of man is the spirit), if history is given the meaning
of "becoming" in a *concordia discors* which does not destroy unity but
contains within itself grounds for a possible unity. Therefore "human
nature" is not to be found in any one particular man but in the whole
history of mankind (and the fact that we naturally use the word
"kind" is significant), while in each single individual are found characteristics made distinct through their difference from the characteristics of
other individuals. The concept of "spirit" in traditional philosophy
and the concept of "human nature" in biology also, should be defined
as "scientific utopias" which are substitutes for the greater utopia
"human nature" sought for in God (and in man, the son of God), and
which indicate the travail of history, rational and emotional hopes,
etc. It is true, of course, that the religions which preached the equality

of men as the sons of God, as well as those philosophies which affirmed man's equality on the basis of his reasoning faculty, were the expressions of complex revolutionary movements (the transformation of the classical world, the transformation of the mediæval world), and that these forged the strongest links in the chain of historical development.

The basis of the latest utopian philosophies, like that of Croce, is that Hegelian dialectics was the last reflection of these great historical links, and that dialectics, the expression of social contradictions, will develop into a pure conceptual dialectic when these contradictions disappear.

In history, real "equality", that is the degree of "spirituality" achieved through the historical development of "human nature", is identified in the system of "public and private", "explicit and implicit" associations that are linked in the "State" and in the world political system; the "equality" here meant is that which is felt as such between the members of an association and the "inequality" felt between different associations; equality and inequality which are of value because there is both individual and group understanding of them. Thus one arrives at the equality or equation between "philosophy and politics", between thought and action, Marxism. All is politics, philosophy as well as the philosophies, and the only "philosophy" is history in action, life itself. It is in this sense that one can interpret the theory of the German proletariat, heir to German classical philosophy, and that it can be affirmed that the theory and elaboration of hegemony by Lenin was also a great "metaphysical" event.

# MARXISM AND MODERN CULTURE

MARXISM has been a potent force in modern culture and, to a certain extent, has determined and fertilised a number of currents of thought within it. The study of this most significant fact has been either neglected or ignored outright by the so-called orthodox (Marxists), and for the following reasons: the most significant philosophical combination that occurred was that in which Marxism was blended with various idealist tendencies, and was regarded by the orthodox, who were necessarily bound to the cultural currents of the last century (positivism, scientism), as an absurdity if not sheer charlatanism. (In his essay on fundamental problems, Plekhanov hints at this but it is only touched upon and no attempt is made at a critical explanation.) Therefore, it seems necessary to evaluate the posing of the problem just as Antonio Labriola attempted to do.

This is what happened: Marxism in fact suffered a double revision, was submitted to a double philosophical combination. On the one hand, some of its elements were absorbed and incorporated, explicitly and implicitly, into various idealist currents (it is enough to cite as examples Croce, Gentile, Sorel, Bergson and the pragmatists); on the other hand, the so-called orthodox, preoccupied with finding a philosophy which, from their very narrow point of view, was more comprehensive than a "simple" interpretation of history, believed they were being orthodox in identifying Marxism with traditional materialism. Still another current turned back to Kant (for example, the Viennese Professor Adler, and the two Italian professors, Alfredo Poggi and Adelchi Baratono). In general one can say that the attempts to combine Marxism with idealist trends stemmed mainly from the "pure" intellectuals, while the orthodox trends were created by intellectual personalities more obviously devoted to practical activity who were, therefore, bound (by more or less close ties) to the masses (something which did not prevent the majority from turning somersaults of some historico-political significance.).

The distinction is very important. The "pure" intellectuals, as elaborators of the most developed ruling-class ideology, were forced to take over at least some Marxist elements to revitalise their own ideas and to check the tendency towards excessively speculative philosophising with the historical realism of the new theory, in order to provide new weapons for the social group to which they were allied.

The orthodox, on the other hand, found themselves battling against religious transcendentalism, the philosophy most widely spread among the masses, and believed they could defeat it with the crudest, most banal materialism, itself a not unimportant layer of common sense, kept alive more than was or is thought by that same religion which finds, among the people, its trivial, base superstitious, sorcery-ridden expression, in which materialism plays no small part.

Why did Marxism suffer the fate of having its principal elements absorbed by both idealism and philosophical materialism? Investigation into this question is sure to be complex and delicate, requiring much subtlety of analysis and intellectual caution. It is very easy to be taken in by outward appearances and to miss the hidden similarities and the necessary but disguised links. The identification of the concepts which Marxism "ceded" to traditional philosophies, and for which they temporarily provided a new lease of life, must be made with careful criticism and means nothing more nor less than rewriting the history of modern thought from the time when Marxism was founded.

Obviously, it is not difficult to trace the clearly defined absorption of ideas, although this, too, must be submitted to a critical analysis. A classic example is Croce's reduction of Marxism to empirical rules for the study of history, a concept which has penetrated even among Catholics . . . and has contributed to the creation of the Italian school of economic-juridical historiography whose influence has spread beyond the confines of Italy. But most needed is the difficult and painstaking search into the "implicit", unconfessed, elements that have been absorbed and which occurred precisely because Marxism existed as a force in modern thought, as a widely diffused atmosphere which modified old ways of thinking through hidden and delayed actions and reactions. In this connection the study of Sorel is especially interesting, because through Sorel and his fate many relevant hints are to be found; the same applies to Croce. But the most important investigation would appear to be of Bergsonian philosophy and of pragmatism, in order to see in full how certain of their positions would have been inconceivable without the historical link of Marxism.

Another aspect of the question is the practical teachings on political science inherited from Marxism by those same adversaries who bitterly combated it on principle in much the same way that the Jesuits, while opposing Machiavelli theoretically, were in practice his best disciples. In an "opinion" published by Mario Missiroli in *La Stampa* when he was its Rome correspondent (about 1925), the writer says something like this: that it remains to be seen whether the more intelligent industrialists are not persuaded in their own minds that *Capital* saw deeply into their affairs and whether they do not make use of the lessons so learned. This would not be surprising in the least, since if Marx made a precise analysis of reality he did no more than systematise rationally and coherently what the historical agents of this reality felt and feel, confusedly and instinctively, and of which they had the greater awareness after his critical analysis.

The other aspect of the question is even more interesting. Why did even the so-called orthodox also "combine" Marxism with other philosophies, and why with one rather than another of those prevalent? Actually the only combination which counts is that made with traditional materialism; the blend with Kantian currents had only a limited success among a few intellectual groups. In this connection, a piece by Rosa Luxemburg on *Advances and Delays in the Development of Marxism* should be looked into; she notes how the constituent parts of this philosophy were developed at different levels but always in accordance with the needs of practical activity. In other words, the founders of the new philosophy, according to her, should have anticipated not only the needs of their own times but also of the times to come, and should have created an arsenal of weapons which could not be used because they were ahead of their times, and which could only be polished up again some time in the future. The explanation is somewhat captious since, in the main, she takes the fact to be explained, restates it in an abstract way, and uses that as an explanation. Nevertheless it contains something of the truth and should be looked into more deeply. One of the historical explanations ought to be looked for in the fact that it was necessary for Marxism to ally itself to alien tendencies in order to combat capitalist hangovers, especially in the field of religion, among the masses of the people.

Marxism was confronted with two tasks: to combat modern ideologies in their most refined form in order to create its own core of independent intellectuals; and to educate the masses of the people whose level of culture was mediæval. Given the nature of the new philosophy the second and basic task absorbed all its strength, both quantitatively and qualitatively. For "didactic" reasons the new philosophy developed in a cultural form only slightly higher than the popular average (which was very low), and as such was absolutely inadequate for overcoming the ideology of the educated classes, despite the fact that the new philosophy had been expressly created to supersede the highest cultural manifestation of the period, classical German philosophy, and in order to recruit into the new social class whose world view it was a group of intellectuals of its own. On the other hand modern culture, particularly the idealist, has been unable to elaborate a popular culture and has failed to provide a moral and scientific content to its own educational programmes, which still remain abstract and theoretical schemes. It is still the culture of a narrow intellectual aristocracy which is able to attract the youth only when it becomes immediately and topically political.

It remains to be seen whether this manner of cultural "deployment" is an historical necessity and whether, always taking into account the circumstances of time and place, it has always been so in the past. The classic example, previous to the modern era, is undoubtedly the Renaissance in Italy and the Reformation in the Protestant countries. In *History of the Baroque Age in Italy* (p.11) Croce writes: "In Italy, its mother and nurse, the Renaissance movement remained aristocratic, confined to select circles; it never broke out of court circles, never penetrated to the people, never became custom and 'prejudice', that is, collective acceptance and faith." The Reformation, on the other hand, "had this virtue of popular penetration but paid for it with the delay in its inner development, by a slow and often interrupted maturing of its vital seed". And on page 8: "And Luther, like the humanists, deprecates sadness and celebrates joy, condemns idleness and commands work but, on the other hand, is led to indifference and hostility to letters and scholarship, so that Erasmus was able to say: '*Ubicumque regnat Lutheranismus, ibi litterarum est interitus*'; and it is true, though not solely as a result of its founder's aversion, that German protestant-ism was almost sterile in scholarship, criticism and philosophy for a couple of centuries. Italian reformers, especially the circle of Giovanni des Valdes and its friends, fused humanism and mysticism, combining the cult of scholarship with moral austerity without effort. Nor did Calvinism, with its hard concept of grace and its strict discipline, encourage free investigation and the cult of beauty; but, through interpreting and explaining and adapting the concept of grace to that of vocation, arrived at an energetic advocacy of the thrifty life, of the production and accumulation of wealth."

Lutheranism and Calvinism inspired a broad popular national move-ment over successive periods during which a higher culture was diffused. Italian reformers inspired no great historical events. It is true that the Reformation in its highest stage of development necessarily assumed Renaissance ways and, like it, spread also to non-Protestant countries where there had been no popular incubation; but the period of popular development made it possible for the protestant countries tenaciously and successfully to resist the crusades by Catholic regi-ments, and it was in this way that the German nation was born as one of the most vigorous of modern Europe. France, which was torn by religious wars in which Catholicism apparently emerged victorious, experienced in the 70's a great popular reform through the Enlighten-ment, Voltairism and the Encyclopædists, which preceded and accompanied the 1789 revolution. Because it embraced the great mass of peasants as well, because it had a clearly defined lay base and tried to substitute for religion an absolutely lay ideology founded on national and patriotic ties, it was in fact a great intellectual and moral reform movement of the French people, more complete than German Lutheranism. But even it had no immediate flowering on a high cultural level, except in political science in the form of a positive science of law.

Marxism assumes this whole cultural past—the Renaissance and the Reformation, German Philosophy, the French Revolution, Calvinism and English classical political economy, lay liberalism and the historical thinking which rests at the foundation of the whole modern conception of life. Marxism crowns the whole movement for intellectual and moral reform dialecticised in the contrast between popular and higher culture. It corresponds to the nexus of Protestant Reformation plus French Revolution. It is philosophy which is also politics, and it is politics which is also philosophy. It is still passing through its popularising stage; to develop a core of independent intellectuals is no simple task but a long process with actions and reactions, agreements and dissolutions and new formations, both numerous and complex; it is the creation of a subordinate social group, without historical initiative, which is constantly growing but in a disorganised manner, never being able to pass beyond a qualitative stage which always lies this side of the possession of State power, of real hegemony over all of society which alone permits a certain organic equilibrium in the development of the intellectual group. Marxism itself has become "prejudice" and "superstition"; as it is, it is the popular aspect of modern historical thinking, but it contains within itself the principle for overcoming this. In the history of culture, which is broader by far than that of philosophy, whenever popular culture has flowered because there was a period of revolt and the metal of a new class was being selected out of the popular mass, there has always been a flowering of "materialism", while conversely the traditional classes have clung to spiritualism. Hegel, astride the French revolution and the Restoration, dialecticised the two streams in the history of thought: materialism and spiritualism, but his synthesis was "a man standing on his head". Those who followed after Hegel destroyed this unity and a return was made to materialist systems of thought on the one hand and on the other, to the spiritual. Marxism, through its founder, relived this whole experience from Hegel to Feuerbach and French materialism in order to reconstitute the synthesis of the dialectical unity—"man on his feet". The mutilation suffered by Hegelian thought was also inflicted on Marxism; on the one hand there has been a return to philosophical materialism and on the other, modern idealist thought has tried to incorporate into itself elements from Marxism which were indispensable to it in its search for a new elixir.

"Politically", the materialist concept is close to the people, to common sense; it is closely bound up with many beliefs and prejudices, with nearly all popular superstitions (sorcery, ghosts, etc.). This can be seen in popular Catholicism and especially in Greek Orthodoxy. Popular religion is crassly materialistic while the official religion of the intellectuals tries to prevent the formation of two distinct religions, two separate strata, in order not to cut itself off from the masses, not to become officially what it is in actuality—the ideology of narrow groups. In this respect, Marxist attitudes must not be confused with those of Catholicism. While the one maintains a dynamic contact with the masses and aims continually to raise new strata of the masses to a higher cultural life, the other maintains a purely mechanical contact, an outer unity based on liturgy and on the cult which most obviously appeals to the masses. Many heretical movements were popular manifestations for a reform of the Church and were efforts to bring it closer to the people, to elevate the people. The Church reacted violently and created the Jesuit Order, armed itself with the decisions of the Council of Trent and organised a marvellous "democratic" apparatus for selecting its intellectuals, but only as single individuals and not as representatives of popular groups.

In the history of cultural developments it is essential to note especially the organisation of culture and also the persons through whom it takes concrete form. In G. de Ruggiero's *Renaissance and Reformation* the attitude of many of the intellectuals led by Erasmus is shown: in the face of the persecutions and articles, they yielded. Therefore the carriers of the Reformation were actually not the intellectuals but the German people as a whole. It is this desertion by the intellectuals when attacked by the enemy which explains the Reformation's "sterility" in the sphere of higher culture, until there gradually emerged a new group of intellectuals from among the masses of the people who remained faithful, and whose work culminated in classical philosophy.

Something similar has happened with Marxism up to the present; the great intellectuals formed in its soil were few in number, not connected with the people, did not come from the people but were the expression of the traditional middle classes to which many reverted during the great historical "turning points". Others remained, but in order to submit the new concept to systematic revision and not to win an independent development for it. The assertion that Marxism is a new, independent original concept and a force in the development of world history is the assertion of the independence and originality of a new culture in birth which will develop with the development of social relations. What exists at each new turn is a varying combination of the old and the new, creating a momentary equilibrium of cultural relationships corresponding to the equilibrium in social relationships. Only after the creation of the State does the cultural problem pose itself in all its complexity and tend towards a concrete solution. In every case, the attitude preceding the State can only be critical-polemical; never dogmatic, it must be romantic in attitude but with a romanticism that consciously aspires towards its own classical composition.

# CRITICAL NOTES ON AN ATTEMPT AT A POPULAR PRESENTATION OF MARXISM BY BUKHARIN

(The "Popular Study" which Gramsci criticises is Bukharin's book *Historical Materialism—a System of Sociology*. This work was first published in Moscow in 1921. As far as is known Gramsci used the French translation of the fourth Russian edition, published in Paris in 1927. Another work which Gramsci mentions in his general criticism of Bukharin's position is the paper on *Theory and Practice from the Standpoint of Dialectic Materialism* read to the International Congress of the History of Science and Technology held in London in 1931.)

## 1. PREMISE

A WORK such as the "Popular Study", destined essentially for a reading public which is not intellectual by profession, ought to have taken as its starting point a critical analysis of the philosophy of common sense, which is the "philosophy of the non-philosopher", that is to say, the world conception absorbed uncritically by various social and cultural circles in which the moral individuality of the average man is developed. Common sense is not a single conception, identical in time and space: it is the "folk-lore" of philosophy and like folk-lore it appears in innumerable forms: its fundamental and most characteristic trait is that of being (even in single brains) disintegrated, incoherent, inconsecutive, in keeping with the social and cultural position of the multitudes whose philosophy it is. When in history a homogeneous social group develops, there also develops, against common sense, a homogeneous, that is, a coherent and systematic philosophy.

The "Popular Study" is mistaken at the outset (implicitly) by presupposing that the great systems of the traditional philosophies and the religion of the high clergy, that is, the world conceptions of the intellectuals and of high culture, are opposed to this development of an original philosophy of the popular masses. In reality these systems are unknown to the multitude and they have no direct effect on their modes of thought and action. This certainly does not mean that they are without any historical effect: but this effect is of another kind. These systems influence the popular masses as an external political force, as an element of force binding together the leading classes, as elements, therefore, of subordination to an external hegemony which limits the original thought of the popular masses negatively, without influencing it positively, like a vital ferment of inmost transformation of what the masses think embryonically and chaotically about the world and about life. The principle elements of common sense are furnished by religion, and so the relationship between religion and common sense is much more intimate than that between common sense and the philosophical systems of the intellectuals. But even as regards religion a critical distinction needs to be made. Every religion, even the Catholic one (or rather, especially the Catholic one, precisely because of its efforts to remain "superficially" unitary in order not to break up into national churches and social stratifications), is in reality a multiplicity of distinct and often contradictory religions: there is the Catholicism of the peasants, the Catholicism of the petty bourgeoisie and of the town workers, the Catholicism of the women and the Catholicism of the intellectuals, and this also is varied and disconnected. But not only do the cruder and less elaborate forms of these various existing Catholicisms have an influence in common sense: previous religions, the earlier forms of present-day Catholicism, popular heretical movements, scientific superstitions bound up with past religions, etc., these have influenced and are components of present-day common sense. In common sense the "realistic", materialistic elements predominate, that is, the direct products of raw sensation; but this does not contradict the religious element; on the contrary; these elements are "superstitious", a-critical. That is why the "Popular Study" represents a danger: it often confirms these a-critical elements, as a result of which common sense still remains ptolemaic, anthropomorphic, anthropocentric, instead of criticising such elements scientifically.

What has been said above about the "Popular Study" which criticises philosophical systems instead of taking as its starting point the criticism of common sense must be understood as a methodological note, and with certain reservations. It certainly does not mean that a criticism of the philosophical systems of the intellectuals should be disregarded. When, individually, a section of the masses critically overcomes common sense, it accepts, by this very fact, a new philosophy: so we see the necessity, in an exposition of Marxism, of polemic against traditional philosophies. Indeed, because of its tendentious character as a mass philosophy, Marxism can only be conceived in a polemical form, in perpetual struggle. Nevertheless, the starting point must still be common sense which is spontaneously the philosophy of the multitudes one is aiming to render ideologically homogeneous.

## 2. GENERAL QUESTIONS

### Historical Materialism and Sociology

One of the preliminary observations is this: that the title does not correspond to the contents of the book. "The theory of Marxism" should mean a logical and coherent systematisation of the philosophical ideas to be met with in various places under the name of Historical Materialism (and which are often spurious, derived from outside and as such ought to be criticised and put an end to). In the first chapters the following questions should be dealt with: What is philosophy? In what sense can a conception of the world be called a philosophy? How does Marxism alter this concept? What is meant by "speculative" philosophy? Could Marxism ever have a speculative form? What are the relationships between ideologies, conceptions of the world, philosophies? How have these relationships been conceived by the traditional philosophies, etc.? The answer to these and other questions constitutes the "theory" of Marxism.

In the "Popular Study" there is also no justification of the premise implied in the exposition and explicitly stated at one place casually, that the *true* philosophy is philosophical materialism and that Marxism is pure "sociology". What does this assertion really mean? If it were true, the theory of Marxism would be philosophical materialism. But in that case what does it mean to say that Marxism is a sociology? What would this sociology be? A science of politics and history? Or a systematic and classified collection, according to a certain order of purely empirical observations of political practice and of the external canons of historical research? We do not find the answers to these questions in the book; still, they alone would be a theory. So the connection between the main title ("Theory", etc.) and the subtitle ("Popular

Study"), is not justified. The subtitle would be a more exact title if the term "sociology" had been given a more circumscribed meaning. In fact the question arises of what is "sociology". Is it not an attempt at a so-called exact (i.e. positivist) science of social facts, that is, of politics and history, i.e. a philosophy in embryo? Has not sociology sought to achieve something similar to Marxism? But we must be clear: Marxism came into existence in the form of aphorisms and practical criteria for a specific case, because its founder (Marx) devoted his intellectual powers to other problems, especially economic ones (in a systematic form), but in these practical criteria and aphorisms is implied a whole conception of the world, a philosophy. Sociology has been an attempt to create a method for historico-political science, dependent on an already elaborated philosophical system (evolutionary positivism), on which sociology has reacted, but only partially. Hence it has become a tendency on its own, it has become a philosophy of the non-philoso-phers, an attempt to describe and classify historical and political facts schematically, according to criteria modelled on the natural sciences. Sociology is therefore an attempt to deduce "experimentally" the laws of evolution of human society in such a way as to be able to "foresee" the future with the same certainty with which one foresees that an oak tree will develop out of an acorn. At the basis of sociology is vulgar evolutionism and it cannot grasp the transition from quantity to quality, a transition which disturbs every evolution and every law of uniformity in the vulgar evolutionist sense. In any case every sociology presupposes a philosophy, a conception of the world, of which it is a subordinate part. And the particular internal "logic" of the various sociologies, through which they acquire mechanical coherence, is not to be confused with the general theory, i.e. the philosophy. This naturally does not mean that research for "laws" of uniformity, is not useful and interesting and that a treatment of direct observations of political practice does not have its *raison d'être*. But we must call a spade a spade and see treatments of this kind for what they are.

All these are "theoretical" problems and not those which Bukharin poses as such. The questions he poses are of an immediate political and ideological kind—ideology in the sense of the intermediary phase between philosophy and everyday practice; they are reflections on particular, disconnected and haphazard historico-political facts. The author does raise one theoretical question at the beginning when he notes a trend of thought which denies the possibility of constructing a sociology from Marxism and maintains that Marxism can only be expressed in concrete historical works.[1] The objection, which is very important, is only resolved in words by the author. Certainly Marxism expresses itself in the concrete study of past history and in the present-day activity of creating new history. But a theory of history and politics can be constructed, since, even if the facts are always individual and changeable in the flux of historical movement, the concepts can be theorised; otherwise one could not even know what movement or the dialectic is, and one would fall into a new form of nominalism.[2]

The reduction of Marxism to a sociology represents the crystallisation of the deteriorating tendencies already criticised by Engels (in his letters to two students published in *Sozial Akademiker*), which consist of reducing a conception of the world into a mechanical formula, giving the impression of having the whole of history in one's pocket. It has been the greatest incentive for the facile journalistic improvisations of superficially "brilliant" men. The experience on which Marxism is based cannot be schematised; it is history itself in its infinite variety and multiplicity, the study of which can lead to "philology" as a method of erudition in the ascertaining of certain facts and to philosophy in the sense of a general methodology of history. This perhaps is what is meant by those writers who, as the *Study* very hurriedly notes in the first chapter, deny that a sociology of Marxism can be constructed, and assert that Marxism only exists in particular historical studies (the assertion, put thus nakedly and crudely, is certainly erroneous, and would be a curious form of nominalism and philosophical scepticism).

To deny that one can construct a sociology, in the sense of a science of society, i.e. a science of history and politics, which is not itself Marxism, only means that one cannot construct an empirical compilation of practical observations which will enlarge the sphere of philology as traditionally understood. If philology is the methodological expression of the importance of ascertaining and specifying

---

[1] Bukharin, *Historical Materialism*, Eng. trans., p. xiv.

[2] The fact that he has not posed correctly the question of what "theory" is, has prevented his posing the question of what religion is and from giving a realistic historical judgment of past philosophies, all of which are presented as delirium and madness.

particular facts in their distinct "individuality", one cannot exclude the practical usefulness of identifying certain more general "laws of tendency" corresponding in politics to statistical laws or to laws of the greatest numbers which have helped the progress of some of the natural sciences. But it has not been emphasised that the statistical law can only be employed in political science and practice in so far as the great mass of the population remains essentially passive—with respect to the questions which interest the historian and the politician—or supposedly remains passive. On the other hand, the extension of statistical laws to the science and practice of politics can have very serious consequences in so far as one assumes them in drawing up perspectives and programmes of action; if in the natural sciences a law (if it is wrong—*Trans.*) can only lead to extraordinary quantities and and blunders which can easily be corrected by fresh research and in any case only make the individual scientist who has used it look ridiculous, in the science and practice of politics it can result in real catastrophes whose damage can never be cleared up. Indeed, in politics the assumption of a statistical law as an essential, fatally operating law is not only a scientific error, but becomes a practical error in action; in addition it encourages mental laziness and programmatic superficiality. It should be observed that political action aims precisely at raising the multitudes out of their passivity, that is, at destroying the laws of the greatest numbers; how then can this be held to be a sociological law? If you think about it, the achievement of a planned or directed economy is itself destined to shatter statistical laws in the mechanical sense (i.e. the product of a haphazard jumble of infinite, arbitrary, individual actions); and although such an economy will have to be based on statistics, it does not, however, mean the same thing: in reality human knowledge is substituted for naturalistic "spontaneity". Another element which in political practice leads to the overthrow of the old naturalistic schemes is the substitution, in a leading function, of collective organisms (parties) for individuals and individual leaders (or divine leaders, as Michels says). With the broadening of mass parties and their organic links with the intimate (economico-productive) life of the masses themselves, the process of standardisation of popular feelings becomes conscious and critical, from being mechanical and haphazard (i.e. produced by existing environmental conditions and similar pressures). The knowledge of these feelings and the final estimate made of them are no longer arrived at through intuition on the part of leaders sustained by the identification of statistical laws, that is to say, through rational and intellectual ways, too often fallacious—which the leader translates into idea-power, into word-power—but they are arrived at through "active and conscious participation", through "sympathy", through first-hand experience of details through a system which could be called "live philology", on the part of the collective organism. In this way a close bond is formed between the large mass, the party and the leading group, and the whole well-co-ordinated complex can move as a "collective-man". . . .

## The Constituent Parts of Marxism

A systematic treatment of Marxism cannot neglect any constituent part of the doctrine of Marx. But in what sense should this be understood? It must deal with all the general philosophical parts, it must therefore develop all the general concepts of a methodology of history and politics, and, in addition, of art, economics and ethics, and it must find the place in the general framework for a theory of the natural sciences. It is very widely held that Marxism is a pure philosophy, the science of dialectics, and that the other parts are economics and politics. As a result it is said that the doctrine is made up of three constituent parts which are at the same time the culmination and superseding of the highest levels reached by the learning of the most advanced European nations around 1848: classical German philosophy, classical English political economy and French political science and activity. This conception, which is more a general examination of the historical sources than a classification arising out of the heart of the doctrine, cannot be maintained as a definitive scheme against any other organisation of the doctrine which may be more close to reality. To the question whether Marxism is not in fact specifically a theory of history, the answer is that this is true, but that politics and economics, even in the specialised phases of political science and practice, and of economic science and policy, cannot be separated from history. That is to say: after carrying out the main task in the general philosophical part—which is Marxism true and proper: the science of dialectics and cognition, to which the general concepts of history, politics and economics are tied in organic unity—it is useful, in a popular study, to present the general ideas of each section or constituent part, and also the extent to which it is a distinct and independent science. Looking into it we see that all these points are at least mentioned in the "Popular Study", but casually, not coherently, in a chaotic and indistinct way, because it lacks any clear and precise idea of what Marxism itself is. . . .

## The Intellectuals

A "well-considered" register should be compiled of the scholars whose opinions are cited or combated at any length, accompanying every name with notes on their significance and scientific importance. (This should also be done for the supporters of Marxism who are certainly not cited in proportion to their originality and significance.) In reality the references to great intellectuals are very fleeting. The question arises: was it not in fact necessary to refer only to the great intellectual opponents and to ignore the secondary ones who only chew over the phrases of the others? We certainly have the impression that Bukharin only wants to attack the weakest people and on their weakest points (or the points most inadequately sustained by the weakest thinkers), in order to win easy verbal victories (since one cannot talk of real victories). He is under the illusion that there is some similarity (apart from the formal and metaphorical one) between the ideological front and the politico-military front. In the political and military struggle it may be good tactics to break through at the points of least resistance in order to be in a position to invest the stronger points with the maximum forces made available by having eliminated the weakest auxiliaries, etc. Political and military victories, within certain limits, have a permanent and universal value, and the strategic end can be attained in a decisive way with general effects for the whole. On the ideological front, however, defeat of the auxiliaries and the minor followers has an almost negligible importance: on this front it is necessary to defeat the eminent people. Otherwise you confuse a newspaper with a book, minor daily polemic with a scientific work; the minor thinkers should be abandoned to the infinite casuistry of journalistic polemic.

A new science achieves the proof of its efficacy and fertile vitality when it shows itself able to face the great champions of the opposing tendencies, when it resolves by itself the vital questions which they posed, and demonstrates incontrovertibly that such questions are false.

It is true that an historical age and a given society are represented rather by the average and therefore mediocre of the intellectuals, but the ideology which is propagated, the mass ideology, must be distinguished from the scientific works and from the great philosophical syntheses which are the real key-stones; these must be clearly overcome, either negatively by showing their baselessness, or positively by opposing to them philosophical syntheses of greater import and significance. Reading the *Study* one gets the impression of a man who cannot sleep because of the moonlight and who exerts himself to kill as many fireflies as he can, convinced that the light will wane or disappear.

## Science and System

Is it possible to write an elementary book, a manual, a "popular study" on a subject which is still at the stage of discussion, polemic and elaboration? A popular manual cannot be imagined except as the formally dogmatic, stylistically settled, scientifically calm exposition of a certain argument; it can only be an introduction to a scientific study, and certainly not an exposition of original scientific research, designed for young people and for a public which from the point of view of scientific ability is still in the first condition of youth and which therefore has a direct need for "certainties", and for opinions which are represented as true and beyond discussion, at least formally. If a certain doctrine has not reached this "classic" phase of its development, any attempt to "manualise" it must necessarily fail and its logical systematisation will only be apparent and illusory; we should see in fact, just as we do in the *Study*, a mechanical justaposition of disparate elements which remain inexorably disconnected and unlinked, despite the unitary veneer given by the literary presentation. Why not, therefore, pose the question in its correct theoretical and historical terms and be content with a book in which a series of essential problems of the doctrine are expounded monographically? This would be more serious and more "scientific". But it is popularly believed that science means "system" and nothing else, and therefore provisional systems are built up which do not have the necessary inner coherence but only the mechanical exterior.

## The Dialectic

In the *Study* there is no treatment whatever of the dialectic. The dialectic is very superficially presupposed and is not expounded, an absurdity in a manual which should contain the essential elements of the doctrine dealt with, and whose bibliographical references should be aimed at stimulating study in order to widen and deepen the argument and not at being a substitute for the manual itself. The absence of a treatment of the dialectic may have two origins: the first may arise from the fact that Marxism is supposed to be split into two parts: a theory of history, and politics seen as sociology, i.e. to be constructed according to the method of the natural sciences (experimental in the shabby positivistic sense), and a philosophy properly so called, which would accordingly be philosophical or metaphysical or mechanical (vulgar) materialism.

Even after the big discussion against mechanicalism, Bukharin does not appear to have very much altered his presentation of the philosophical problem. As appears from the memoir presented to the London Congress on the History of Science, he continues to maintain that Marxism is divided into two parts: the doctrine of history and politics, and the philosophy, which, however, he now says is dialectical materialism and no longer the old philosophical materialism. Put in this way he no longer understands the importance and significance of the dialectic, which is degraded from being a doctrine of consciousness and the inner substance of history and the science of politics, into being a subspecies of formal logic and elementary scholasticism. The rôle and significance of the dialectic can be conceived in all their profundity only if Marxism is seen as an integral and original philosophy which initiates a new phase of history and of the development of world thought, in so far as it supersedes (and at the same time includes into itself the vital elements of), both idealism and materialism, the traditional expressions of former societies. If Marxism is only thought of as subordinate to another philosophy, one cannot conceive of the new dialectic; it is precisely in this that the victory effects and expresses itself.

The second origin appears to be of a psychological character. It is felt that the dialectic is very arduous and difficult, in that dialectical thinking goes against vulgar common sense which is dogmatic, hungering after incontrovertible certainties and expresses itself in formal logic. To understand this attitude better one can think what would happen if the natural and physical sciences were taught in primary and secondary schools on the basis of Einstein's theory of relativity and if the traditional notions of the "laws of nature" were accompanied by the notion of statistical laws or laws of the greatest numbers. The children would understand nothing about anything and the clash between school teaching and family and popular life would be so great that the school would become an object of scorn and sceptical caricature.

This motive seems to me to act as a brake on Bukharin; he in fact capitulates before common sense and vulgar thought because he has not posed the problem to himself in correct theoretical terms and therefore in practice is unarmed and impotent. The rough uneducated environment has dominated the educator, vulgar common sense has imposed itself on science and not vice versa; if environment is the educator it must in its turn be educated, but the *Study* does not understand this revolutionary dialectic. At the root of all the mistakes of the *Study* and of its author (whose position has not changed even after the big discussion which seems to have led him to repudiate his book, as appears from his memoir presented at the London Congress) lies precisely this pretence of dividing Marxism into two parts: a "sociology", and a systematic philosophy. Cut off from the theory of history and politics, philosophy can only be metaphysics, whereas the great achievement in the history of modern thought represented by Marxism is precisely the concrete historicisation of philosophy and its identification with history. . . .

### The Concept of "Science"

Posing the problem as a search for laws, for regular, uniform, constant lines, is linked with the need, looked at in a somewhat child-like and naïve way, of peremptorily resolving the practical problem of the foreseeability of historical events. Since, by a strange turning upside down of perspectives, it "seems" that the natural sciences provide the ability to foresee the evolution of natural processes, historical methodology has been conceived as "scientific" only if, and in so far as, it enables one abstractly to "foresee" the future of society. Hence the search for essential causes, or rather for the "first cause", the "cause of causes". But the *Theses on Feuerbach* have already anticipated and criticised this naïve conception. In reality one can foresee only the struggle and not its concrete episodes; these must be the result of opposing forces in continuous movement, never reducible to fixed quantities, because in them quantity is always becoming quality. Really one "foresees" to the extent to which one acts, to which one makes a voluntary effort and so contributes concretely to creating the "foreseen" result. Foresight reveals itself therefore not as a scientific act of knowledge, but as the abstract expression of the effort one makes, the practical method of creating a collective will.

How could foresight be an act of knowledge? One knows what has been and what is, not what will be, what is "non-existent", and so unknowable by definition. Foresight is therefore only a practical act which, in so far as it is not futile or a waste of time, can have no other explanation than that stated above. The problem of the foreseeability of historical events needs to be posed correctly, so that an exhaustive criticism can be made of mechanical causation, in order to deprive it of all scientific prestige and reduce it to a mere myth which was perhaps useful in the past in a backward period of development of certain subordinate social groups.

But it is the concept of "science" itself, arising from the "Popular Study", which needs to be critically destroyed: it is taken directly from the natural sciences as if these were the only science, or science *par excellence*, as has been decided by positivism. But in the "Popular Study" the term science has many meanings, some explicit, others understood and scarcely mentioned. The explicit meaning is the one that "science" has in physical research. At other times it seems that method is indicated. But does there exist a general method and if it exists can it mean anything other than a philosophy? At other times it could mean simply formal logic, but can this be called a method and a science? The point must be settled that every research has its own determined method and constructs its own determined science, and that the method is developed and has been elaborated together with the development and elaboration of that determined research and science with which it is one. To believe that one piece of scientific research can be advanced by applying a typical method, chosen because it has yielded good results in other research to which it was appropriate, is a strange mistake, which has little in common with science. But there are also some general criteria which can be said to constitute the critical conscience of any scientist, whatever his "specialisation", which must be spontaneously on guard in his work. Thus a man cannot be called a scientist who shows little trust in his particular criteria, who does not have a full understanding of the concepts used, who has little information and understanding of the earlier state of the problems dealt with, who is not very cautious in his assertions, who does not advance in a necessary but in an arbitrary way and without linking the steps together, who is unable to recognise the gaps existing in the accomplishments of his own work, but ignores them and contents himself with purely verbal solutions or connections instead of declaring that he is dealing with provisional statements which can be taken up and developed, etc.

One point which can be made about many polemical references in the *Study* is their systematic refusal to recognise the possibility of error on the part of the individual writers cited; because of this the most varied opinions and the most contradictory wishes are attributed to a social group of which the scholars are always taken as the representatives. This point is tied up with more general methodological criteria; in other words, it is not very "scientific", or more simply, "very serious", to choose one's adversaries from among the most stupid and mediocre, or again, to choose the least essential and most incidental of their opinions and presume that one has "entirely demolished" the opponent because one has demolished one of his secondary or minor opinions, or that one has demolished an ideology or a doctrine because one has shown the theoretical insufficiency of its third- or fourth-rate champions. Again: "one must be just with one's opponents", in the sense that one must make the effort to understand what they really meant and not stop maliciously at the superficial and obvious meanings of their words. This must be said if the end proposed is to raise the tone and intellectual level of one's followers and not just the immediate one of surrounding oneself with a desert by any means or in any fashion. It must be posed from this point of view: that one's follower must discuss and maintain his point of view in discussion with able and intelligent opponents and not merely with crude uneducated people who are convinced in an "authoritarian" or "emotional" way. The possibility of errors must be stated and justified, without in any way weakening one's own conception by this, because what matters is not the opinion of Titus, Caius or Sempronius but that totality of opinions which have become collective, an element and force in society: these must be confuted, in their most representative theoreticians, men who are moreover worthy of respect for the elevation of their thought and for their immediate "disinterestedness", but not because one thinks that by doing this one has "demolished" the corresponding social element and force (which would be pure enlightened rationalism), but because one has contributed: (1) to maintaining one's own side and strengthening the spirit of distinctiveness and separation; (2) to creating the basis for one's own side to absorb and bring to life its own original doctrine corresponding to its own conditions of life. . . .

### The so-called "reality of the external world"

The whole polemic against the subjectivist conception of reality, with the "terrible" question of "the reality of the external world", is posed badly, conducted worse and is in great part futile and useless. (I am referring also to the memoir presented to the Congress of the History of Science, held in London in June-July, 1931). From the point of view of a "popular study" the whole treatment answers more to an itch for intellectual pedantry than to logical necessity. The general public does not even believe that one can even pose such a problem as to whether the external world exists objectively. It is sufficient to state the problem to hear an uncontrollable and gargantuan outburst of hilarity. The public "believes" that the external world is objectively real, but it is precisely here that the question arises: what is the origin of this "belief" and what critical value does it have objectively? In fact this belief is of religious origin even if the people who share it are indifferent to religion. Since all religions have taught that the world, nature, the universe were created by God before the creation of man and that man therefore found the world already prepared, catalogued and defined once for all, this belief has become an iron datum of "common sense" and persists with the same firmness even if the religious sentiment is exhausted and dormant. That is why basing oneself on this experience of common sense in order to demolish the subjectivist view with "laughter", has a rather "reactionary" significance of a return to religious sentiment; in fact Catholic writers and speakers resort to the same means in order to obtain the same effect of caustic ridicule.[1] In the memoir presented to the London Congress, Bukharin implicitly answers this point (which is of an external character, though it has its importance) by noting that Berkeley, to whom we owe the first complete statement of the subjectivist conception, was a bishop (so it seems we must deduce the religious origins of the theory) and then by saying that only an "Adam" who found himself for the first time in the world could think that the world existed only because he thought it (here also the religious origin of the theory is insinuated, but with little or no power of conviction).

It seems to me that the problem is rather this: how can it be explained that such a conception, which is certainly not futile even for a Marxist, if expounded in public today, can only provoke laughter and grimaces? It seems a typical case of the distance which has grown up between science and life, between certain intellectual groups, even those at the "central" leadership of high culture, and the great popular masses: and how the language of philosophy has become a jargon with as much effect as that of Harlequin. But if "common sense" is exalted, the Marxist should at the same time seek an explanation of the real significance of the conception, and of why it originated and came to be propagated among the intellectuals, and also of why it arouses the laughter of common sense. Certainly the subjectivist conception belongs to modern philosophy in its most complete and advanced form, if from it, and as the overcoming of it, there arose historical materialism which poses, in the theory of the superstructure, in realistic and historical language what traditional philosophy used to express in speculative language. The demonstration of this assumption, which is here hardly mentioned, would be of the greatest cultural import, because it would put an end to a series of discussions, as futile as they are useless and would permit an organic development of Marxism up to the point where it was made into the hegemonic exponent of high

---

[1] The Church (through the Jesuits and especially the neo-scholastics: University of Louvain and the Sacred Heart at Milan) has sought to absorb positivism and also to use this reasoning in order to ridicule the idealists with the public: "The idealists are those who think that this tower exists only because you think it; if you did not think it the tower would cease to exist."

culture. It is a wonder that the connection between the idealist assertion that the reality of the world is a creation of the human spirit, and the assertion of the historicity and mortality of all ideologies on the part of Marxism, since ideologies are the expressions of the structure and are modified with its modification, has never been asserted and appropriately developed.

The question is closely connected—naturally—with the question of the so-called exact or physical sciences and the position almost of a fetish, or rather of the only true philosophy or knowledge of the world, which they have come to assume in the framework of Marxism.

But what is to be understood by the subjectivist conception of reality? Could one take it to be stated in any one of the many subjectivist theories worked out by a whole series of philosophers and professors up to the solipsistic theories? The fact is that Marxism, in this case as well, must be related to Hegelianism, which represents the most complete and brilliant form of this conception, and that from the later theories only some partial aspects and instrumental values are to be taken into consideration. And it will be necessary to examine the weird forms which the conception has assumed among its followers as well as in its more or less intelligent critics. Thus what Tolstoy writes in his *Childhood and Youth* should be recalled: Tolstoy tells that he was so enthusiastic about the subjectivist conception of reality, that he was often dizzy because he used to turn round suddenly, convinced that he would be able to catch the moment when he would see nothing because his spirit had not had time to "create" reality (or something similar: the extract from Tolstoy is characteristic and very interesting from the literary point of view).[1]

---

[1] cf. Tolstoy, *Childhood, Boyhood and Youth* (ed. Oxford Classics) p. 196: "But by none of my philosophical tendencies was I so carried away as by scepticism, which at one time led me to the verge of insanity. I imagined that besides myself nobody and nothing existed in the universe, that objects were not objects at all, but images which appeared only when I paid attention to them, and that as soon as I left off thinking of them, these images immediately disappeared. In a word, I coincided with Schelling in the conviction that not objects exist but my relation to them. There were moments when, under the influence of this *idée fixe*, I reached such a state of insanity that I sometimes looked rapidly round to one side, hoping to catch emptiness (*néant*) unawares where I was not." In addition to the example of Tolstoy, recall the witty form in which a journalist represents the "professional or traditional philosopher" (presented by Croce in the chapter on The Philosophers) who remains for years seated at his desk, staring at the ink-pot and wondering: "Is this ink-pot *inside me* or *outside me*?"

It requires to be shown that the "subjectivist" conception, having served to criticise transcendental philosophy from one side, as well as the simple metaphysics of common sense and of philosophical materialism, can find its true nature and its historical interpretation only within the conception of the superstructure, whereas in its speculative form it is nothing but mere philosophical romance.

The point which must be made about the "Popular Study" is that it has presented the subjectivist conception as it appears from the criticism of common sense and that it has taken up the conception of the reality of the external world in its most trivial and a-critical form, without even suspecting that the charge of mysticism could be brought against it, as in fact was done.[1] We have only to analyse this conception to see that it is not very easy to justify a point of view of external objectivity thus mechanically understood. Does it seem that there can exist an extra-historical and extra-human objectivity? Who will judge this objectivity? Who can put himself into this position of knowing things from "the point of view of the cosmos in itself" and what would such a point of view signify? It can very well be argued that we are dealing with a residue of the concept of God, precisely in its mystical conception of an unknown God. Engels' formulation that "the unity of the world consists in its materiality demonstrated . . . by a long and laborious development of philosophy and the natural sciences", contains the very germ of the correct conception, because it appeals to history and to man in order to prove objective reality. Objective always means "humanly objective", what may correspond exactly to "historically subjective", in other words objective would mean "universally subjective". Man knows objectively in so far as his knowledge is real for the whole of mankind *historically* unified in a unitary cultural system; but this process of historical unification takes place with the disappearance of the internal contradictions which tear human society apart, contradictions which are the condition for the formation of groups and the emergence of ideologies which are not concretely universal but are rendered immediately short-lived by the practical origin of their substance. There is, therefore, a struggle towards objectivity (towards being free from partial and fallacious ideologies) and this struggle is

[1] In the memoir presented to the London Congress, Bukharin noted the accusation of mysticism, attributing it to Sombart and contemptuously ignoring it: Sombart certainly took it from Croce.

itself the struggle for the cultural unification of mankind. What the idealists call "spirit" is not a point of departure but of arrival, the totality of superstructures in development towards unification which is concrete, objectively universal, and not just a unitary presupposition, etc.

Experimental science has offered the basis on which this cultural unity has, up till now, attained its greatest extension: it has been the aspect of knowledge which has contributed most towards unifying the "spirit" and rendering it universal; it is the most concretely objectivised and universalised subjectivity.

The concept of "objective" in metaphysical materialism appears to mean an objectivity which exists even outside of man, but to assert that reality would exist even if man did not exist is either to state a metaphor or to fall into a form of mysticism. We know reality only in its relations with man, and just as man is an historical process of becoming, so also knowledge and reality are a becoming, and objectivity is a becoming, etc.

Engels' expression that "the materiality of the world is demonstrated by the long and laborious development of philosophy and the natural sciences" needs to be analysed and made precise. By science does he mean the theoretical or the practical-experimental activity of the scientists or the synthesis of the two activities? In this we could be said to have the typical unitary process of reality, in the experimental activity of the scientist which is the first model of the dialectical mediation between man and nature, the elementary historical cell by which man, putting himself into relation with nature through technology, knows it and controls it. Undoubtedly, the promulgation of the experimental method separates two worlds of history, two epochs, and begins the process of the dissolution of theology and metaphysics and the development of modern thought, whose crowning is Marxism. Scientific method is the first cell of the new method of production, of the new form of active union between man and nature. The scientist-experimenter is also a worker, not a pure thinker, and his thought is continually controlled by practice and *vice versa*, up to the point where a perfect unity of theory and practice is formed.

The neo-scholastic Casotti (Mario Casotti, *Teacher and Scholar*) writes: "The researches of the naturalists and the biologists presuppose an already existing life and real organism," an expression which comes near to that of Engels in *Anti-Dühring*.

The agreement between Catholicism and Aristotelianism on the question of the objectivity of reality.

In order to understand exactly the possible significance of the problem of the reality of the external world, it may be useful to develop the example of the notions of "East" and "West" which do not stop being "objectively real" even if on analysis they prove to be nothing but conventions, i.e. "historico-cultural constructions" (often the terms "artificial" and "conventional" indicate "historical" facts, produced by the development of civilisation and not just rationally arbitrary or individually artificial constructions). The example given by Bertrand Russell in his little book should be recalled. Russell says roughly the following: "Without the existence of man on earth, we cannot think of the existence of London and Edinburgh, but we can think of the existence of two points in space where London and Edinburgh are today, one to the North and the other to the South." It could be objected that without thinking of the existence of man one cannot think of "thinking", one cannot think in general of any fact or relationship which exists only in so far as man exists. What would North-South or East-West mean without man? These are real relationships but nevertheless they would not exist without man and without the development of civilisation. It is evident that East and West are arbitrary, conventional, i.e. historical, constructions, because outside real history any point on the earth is East and West at the same time. We can see this more clearly from the fact that these terms have been crystallised not from the point of view of man in general but from the point of view of the cultured European classes who, through their world hegemony, have made the terms evolved by themselves accepted everywhere. Japan is the Far East not only for Europe but perhaps also for an American from California and for the Japanese themselves, who through English political culture will call Egypt the Near East. Thus through the historical content which has been compounded with the geographical term, the expressions East and West have ended by meaning certain relationships between complexes of different civilisations. So Italians often speak of Morocco as an "oriental" country, in order to refer to its Moslem and Arab civilisation. However, these references are real, they correspond to real facts, they will allow one to travel over land and sea and reach a known destination, to "forsee" the future, to objectivise reality, to understand the objectivity of the external world. The rational and the real are identified.

It seems that without understanding this relationship one cannot understand Marxism, its position *vis-à-vis* idealism and mechanical materialism, and the importance and significance of the doctrine of the superstructure. It is not correct to say that in Marxism the Hegelian "Idea" is replaced by the "concept" of structure, as Croce asserts. The Hegelian "Idea" is resolved into the structure as much as into the superstructures and the whole method of conceiving philosophy has been "historicised"; in other words, the emergence of a new kind of philosophy, more concrete and historical than its predecessor, has begun.

NOTE: The standpoint of Professor Lukacs regarding Marxism needs to be examined. It seems that Lukacs asserts that one can only speak of the dialectic for the history of man but not for nature. He may be right and he may be wrong. If his assertion presupposes a dualism between nature and man he is wrong, because he falls into a view of nature proper to religion and Greco-Christian philosophy and also into idealism, which in reality does not manage to unite men and nature and relate them together other than verbally. But if human history should be conceived also as the history of nature (also through the history of science), how can the dialectic be separated from nature? Perhaps Lukacs, in reaction against the baroque theories of the "Popular Study", has fallen into the opposite error, into a form of idealism.

## Judgment of Past Philosophies

The superficial criticism of subjectivism in the "Popular Study" leads into a more general question, that of the standpoint taken regarding past philosophies and philosophers. To judge the whole philosophical past as madness and folly is not only an anti-historical error, since it contains the anachronistic pretence that in the past they should have thought like today, but it is a truly genuine hangover of metaphysics, since it supposes a dogmatic thought valid at all times and in all countries, by whose standard one should judge all the past. Anti-historical method is nothing but metaphysics. The fact that philosophical systems have been suspended does not exclude the fact that they were historically valid and carried out a necessary function: their short-livedness should be considered from the point of view of the entire historical development and of the real dialectic; that they *deserved* to perish is neither a moral judgment nor sound thinking emerging from an "objective" point of view, but a dialectical-historical judgment. One can compare this with Engels' presentation of the Hegelian proposition that "all that is rational is real and all that is real is rational", a proposition which will be valid for the past as well.

In the *Study* the past is judged as "irrational" and "monstrous" and the history of philosophy becomes the historical treatment of teratology, since he starts from a metaphysical point of view. (In fact the *Communist Manifesto* contains the highest praise of the dying world.) If this way of judging the past is a theoretical error and a deviation from Marxism, can it have any educational significance, will it generate activity? It does not appear so, because the question would reduce itself to presuming that one is a special person simply because one was born in the present time and not in a past century. But at every time there has been a past and a present and being "up to date" is praise only for jokes.[1]

### Immanence and Marxism

In the *Study* it is noted that the terms "immanence" and "immanent" are certainly used in Marxism, but that "evidently" this use is only "metaphorical". Very good. But has he in any way explained what immanence and immanent mean "metaphorically"? Why have these terms continued to be used and not replaced? Purely out of a horror of creating new words? Usually when one new conception of the world succeeds another, the earlier language continues to be used but is used metaphorically. All language is a continuous process of metaphors, and the history of semantics is an aspect of the history of culture: language is at the same time a living thing and a museum of the fossils

---

[1] The story is told of a French petty bourgeois who had the word "contemporary" printed on his visiting card: he thought he was nothing and one day discovered that he was in fact something, precisely a "contemporary".

of life and civilisation. When I use the word *disaster* no one can accuse me of astrological beliefs, and when I say "By Jove", no one can believe that I am a worshipper of the pagan divinity; nevertheless, these expressions are a proof that modern civilisation is a development of both paganism and astrology. The term "immanence" in Marxism has its precise meaning which is hidden in the metaphor and this must be defined exactly; in reality this definition would truly have been "theory". Marxism continues the philosophy of immanence, but rids it of all its metaphysical trimmings and leads it on to the concrete basis of history. The use is metaphorical only in the sense that the former immanence is superseded, has been superseded, although it is still pre-supposed as a link in the process of thought from which the new link has been born. On the other hand, is the new concept of immanence completely new? It appears that in Giordano Bruno, for example, there are many examples of such a new conception; Marx and Engels knew about Bruno. They knew about him and there remain traces of Bruno's works in their notes. Conversely, Bruno was not without influence on classical German philosophy, etc. Here are many problems in the history of philosophy which could be usefully examined.

The question of the relationship between language and metaphor is not simple, far from it. Language, however, is always metaphorical. If it is perhaps not correct to say that every statement is metaphorical in respect of the thing or the material and tangible object indicated (or the abstract concept), since that would broaden too much the concept of metaphor, it can still be said that present-day language is metaphorical in respect of the meanings and ideological content which the words have had in earlier periods of civilisation. A book on semantics—that of Michel Breals, for example—provides an historically and critically reconstituted catalogue of the semantic changes of certain groups of words. Many errors both in the field of learning and of practice derive from not taking account of this fact, in other words from not having a critical and historical view of the phenomenon of language: (1) An error of an æsthetic character, which today is being to some extent corrected but which was in the past a ruling doctrine, is that of re-garding as "beautiful" in themselves certain expressions as distinct from others in so far as they are crystallised metaphors; the rhetoricians and grammarians swoon at certain words, in which they discover who knows how much virtue and abstract artistic essence. The very bookish philologist's word "joy", which suffers agonies as a result of certain etymological or semantic analyses, is actually confused with artistic delight: recently we had the pathological case of *Language and Poetry* by Giulio Bertoni. (2) A practical error which has many followers is the utopian idea of a fixed universal language. (3) An arbitrary tendency towards absurd word innovations, which arises from the problem posed by Pareto and the pragmatists regarding "language as the cause of error". Pareto, like the pragmatists in so far as they believe that they have created a new conception of the world, or at least that they have originated a certain science (and that they have therefore given words a new significance or at least a new shade of meaning, or that they have created new concepts), finds himself faced with the fact that traditional words, especially those in common use, but also those used by the cultured classes and even those used by specialist groups dealing with the same science, continue to keep their old meaning despite the innovation of content, and this has reactions. Pareto creates his own "dictionary", demonstrating his aim of creating his own "pure" or "mathematical" language. The pragmatists theorise abstractly about language as the cause of error (see G. Prezzolini's little book). But is it possible to rid language of its broad metaphorical meanings? It is impossible. Language is transformed together with the transformation of the whole of civilisation, through the flowering into culture of new classes, through the hegemony exercised by one national language on others, etc., and in point of fact continues to use metaphorically the words of preceding cultures and civilisations. No one today thinks that the word "dis-aster" is bound up with astrology, and those who use it in this way are considered to be wrong. In the same way an atheist can speak of "disgrace"[1] without being thought a follower of predestination, etc. The new "metaphorical" significance broadens with the broadening of the new culture, which, on the other hand, also coins new words and borrows words from other languages and uses them with a precise significance, i.e. without the broad aura they had in the original language. So it is probable that the term "immanence" is known, understood and used by many people for the first time only in the new "metaphorical" significance given to it by Marxism.

[1] The Italian word *disgrazia* means a misfortune, an accident.

## Questions of Nomenclature and Content

One of the characteristics of intellectuals as a socially crystallised category (one which, in other words, sees itself developing uninterruptedly in history and therefore as independent of the struggle of groups, and not as the expression of a dialectical process through which every ruling social group puts forward its own category of intellectuals), is precisely their reuniting, in the ideological sphere, with an earlier intellectual category by using the same nomenclature for concepts. Every new historical organism (type of society) creates a new superstructure, whose specialised representatives and standard bearers (the intellectuals) must also be seen as "new" intellectuals, arising from the new situation, and not as a continuation of the preceding intellectuality. If the "new" intellectuals see themselves as a direct continuation of the preceding "intelligentsia" they are not in fact "new", that is, they are not tied to the new social group which represents organically the new historical situation, but are rather a conservative and fossilised residue of the historically superseded social group (which may be the same thing as saying that the new historical situation has not yet reached the level of development necessary to have the capacity of creating new superstructures, but still lives inside the crumbling casing of former history). Nevertheless, we must take account of the fact that no historical situation, even that due to the most radical change, completely transforms language, at least in its external, formal aspects. But the content of language must be changed, even if it is difficult to have exact immediate knowledge of it. On the other hand, the phenomenon is historically complex and complicated because of the existence of different cultures typical of the different strata of the new social group, some of which, in the ideological field, are still buried in the culture of historical situations sometimes even earlier than those most recently superseded. A class some of whose strata still retain a ptolemaic conception of the world, can still be the representative of a very advanced historical situation; ideologically backward (at least for some parts of its conception of the world, which is still disjointed and ingenuous), these strata are still the most advanced in practice, i.e. in their economic and political rôle. If the task of the intellectuals is that of determining and organising moral and intellectual reform, that is, of adjusting culture to the practical function, it is evident that "crystal-lised" intellectuals are conservative and reactionary. For whereas the new social group at least feels that it is separate and distinct from the preceding one, they do not even feel this distinction, but think that they can tie themselves up with the past.

On the other hand, I do not say that the entire inheritance of the past should be rejected: there are some "instrumental values" which must be accepted as a whole in order to continue to be elaborated and refined. But how can we distinguish an instrumental value from a short-lived philosophical value which ought without doubt to be rejected? It often happens that, because a short-lived philosophical value of a certain past trend is accepted, an instrumental value of another trend is rejected because it contradicts the former, even if this instrumental value would have been useful in expressing the new cultural and historical content.

So we see the term "materialism" accepted together with its past content, and on the other hand the term "immanence" is rejected because in the past it had a certain cultural and historical content. The difficulty of adjusting literary expression to the conceptual content, and the confusion of questions of terminology with questions of sub-stance and *vice versa*, is characteristic of philosophical dilettantism, of a lack of historical sense in collating different stages of cultural develop-ment, i.e. of an anti-dialectical, dogmatic conception, imprisoned by abstract schemes of formal logic.

The term "materialism" in the first fifty years of the nineteenth century must be understood not only in the narrow, technical philo-sophical sense, but in the wider significance which it was coming to assume polemically in the discussions which began with the rise and victorious development of modern culture. Any philosophical doctrine was called materialism which excluded transcendence from the domain of thought; and therefore, in reality, not only all pantheism and immanentism was given the name of materialism but it was also applied to any practical standpoint inspired by political realism, which was opposed, in other words, to the inferior trends of political romanticism like the popularised doctrines of Mazzini, which only spoke of "mis-sions", of "ideals" and other similarly vague, nebulous ideas and senti-mental abstractions. Even nowadays in Catholic polemics the term materialism is often used in this sense; materialism is the opposite of spiritualism in the narrow sense, i.e. of religious spiritualism and so in it is comprised the whole of Hegelianism and the classical German philosophy in general, in addition to French sensationalism and illuminism. So, in the terms of common sense, everything which aims at finding the end of life in this earth and not in paradise is called materialism. All economic activity which left behind the limits of mediæval production was "materialism" because it seemed an "end in itself", economy for economy's sake, activity for activity's sake, in the same way as today for the average European America is "materialist", because the use of machines and the number of factories and businesses exceeds a certain limit which to the average European appears "right", that within which "spiritual" needs are not mortified. And so a polemical twist of feudal culture against the developing bourgeoisie is actually used today by European bourgeois culture, on the one side against a more developed capitalism than the European, and on the other against the practical activity of subordinate social groups for whom, initially and for a whole historical epoch (i.e. until they have constructed their own economy and their own social structure) activity must be prevalently economic, or at least expressed in economic and structural terms. Traces of this conception of materialism remain in language: in German *geistlich* also means "clerical", pertaining to the clergy, as also in the Russian *dukhoviez*; and that this is prevalent can be deduced from many Marxist writers for whom, correctly, religion, theism, etc., are the points of reference for recognising "consistent materialists".

One of the reasons, and perhaps the main one, for the reduction of historical materialism to traditional metaphysical materialism is to be sought in the fact that historical materialism had to be a predominantly critical and polemical phase of philosophy, so long as there was a need for an already complete and perfect system. But complete and perfect systems are always the work of individual philosophers, and in these, side by side with the actual historical part, i.e. that corresponding to the contemporary conditions of life, there is always an abstract, "a-historic" part, in the sense that it is bound up with the preceding philosophies and answers the external and pedantic needs of the architecture of the system, or is due to personal idiosyncracies; for this reason the philosophy of a period cannot be any one individual or

tendentious system: it is the totality of all the individual and tendentious philosophies, plus scientific opinions, plus religion and plus
common sense. Can a system of such a kind be formed artificially?
Through the work of individuals and groups? Critical activity is the
only possibility, especially in the sense of passing and solving critically
the problems which are presented as expressions of historical development. But the first of these problems which must be stated and understood is this: that the new philosophy cannot be in complete harmony
with any system of the past, whatever this is called. Identity of terms
does not mean identity of concepts.

A book to be studied in relation to this argument is F. A. Lange's
*History of Materialism*. This work will be more or less superseded by
later studies of individual materialist philosophers, but its cultural importance remains unimpaired, from this point of view: a whole series
of followers of historical materialism referred to it for information
about their predecessors and to find out the fundamental concepts of
materialism. We can say that the following is what happened, schematically: they started with the dogmatic presupposition that historical
materialism is undoubtedly traditional materialism somewhat revised
and amended (amended by the "dialectic", which thus came to be
assumed as a chapter of formal logic and not as itself a logic, that is, a
theory of knowledge): in Lange they studied what traditional materialism was and its concepts were taken as the concepts of historical
materialism. So it can be said that for the greater part of the body of
concepts which are put forward under the label of historical materialism, the principal teacher and founder was none other than Lange.
That is why the study of this book is of great cultural and critical
interest, all the more since Lange is a conscientious and acute historian
who has a very precise, definite and limited conception of materialism,
and therefore, to the great amazement and almost scorn of some (like
Plekhanov), considered neither historical materialism nor the philosophy of Feuerbach to be materialism. Here also we can see how conventional is terminology, but it has its importance in causing errors
and deviations when one forgets that it is always necessary to go back
to the cultural sources in order to identify the exact value of the concepts, since different shaped heads can wear the same cap. It is noteworthy, on the other hand, that Marx never called his conception

"materialist", and how, when speaking of French materialism, he criticised it and stated that the criticism ought to have been more exhaustive. Thus he never uses the formula of "materialist dialectic" but spoke of "rational" as opposed to "mystic", which gives the term "rational" a very precise significance.

## The Concept of "Orthodoxy"

From some points developed earlier it appears that the concept of "orthodoxy" must be renewed and brought back to its authentic origins. Orthodoxy must not be looked for in this or that follower of Marxism, in this or that tendency linked by extraneous currents to the original doctrine, but in the fundamental concept that Marxism, "sufficient to itself", contains in itself all the fundamental elements not only for constructing a whole and integral conception of the world, a total philosophy and a theory of the natural sciences, but also for bringing to life an integral practical organisation of society; in other words, for becoming a total, integral civilisation.

Renewed in this way, the concept of orthodoxy helps to make more precise the adjective "revolutionary", which is usually applied with such facility to different conceptions of the world, theories, philosophies. Christianity was revolutionary as against paganism because it was an element of complete break between the supporters of the old and the new worlds. A theory is in fact "revolutionary" to the extent to which it is an element of separation and conscious distinction into two camps, in so far as it is an inaccessible peak for the opposing camp. To hold that Marxism is not a completely autonomous and independent structure of thought, antagonistic to all traditional philosophies and religions, means in reality not to have cut one's bonds with the old world, if not actually to have capitulated to it. Marxism has no need of heterogeneous supports; it is itself sufficiently robust and so productive of new truths that the old world resorts to it to furnish its arsenal with the most modern and effective arms. This signifies that Marxism is beginning to exercise its own hegemony over traditional culture, but the latter, which is still robust and above all is more refined and finished, tries to react like conquered Greece, to stop the crude Roman conqueror from being victorious.

# THE FORMATION OF INTELLECTUALS

ARE intellectuals an autonomous and independent social class or does every social class have its own specialised category of intellectuals? The problem is complex because of the various forms taken by the real historical process of the formation of different categories of intellectuals.

The most important of these forms are two-fold:

(1) Every social class, coming into existence on the original basis of an essential function in the world of economic production, creates with itself, organically, one or more groups of intellectuals who give it homogeneity and consciousness of its function not only in the economic field but in the social and political field as well: the capitalist *entrepreneur* creates with himself the industrial technician, the political economist, the organiser of a new culture, of a new law, etc. It should be noted that the capitalist represents a higher elaboration of society, already characterised by a certain leading and technical (i.e. intellectual) capacity: in addition to having a certain technical capacity in the sphere circumscribed by his activity and initiative he must also have it in other spheres, at least in those nearest to economic production (he must be an organiser of masses of men; he must be an organiser of the "confidence" of the investors in his business, of the purchasers of his goods, etc.).

If not all capitalists, at least an *élite* of them must have the capacity for organising society in general, in all its complex organism of duties up to the State organism, because of the need to create the most favourable conditions for the expansion of their own class—or they must at least have the capacity to choose "officers" (specialised employees) to entrust with this activity of organising the general relations outside their enterprises.

It can be seen that the "organic" intellectuals which each new class creates with itself and elaborates in its own progressive development are for the most part "specialisations" of partial aspects of the primitive activity of the new social type which the new class has brought to light.

Feudal lords as well possessed a particular technical ability: military ability; and it is precisely from the moment when the aristocracy loses its monopoly of technical-military ability that the crisis of feudalism begins. But the formation of intellectuals in the feudal world and in the earlier classical world is a question to be examined apart: these formations and elaborations follow paths and methods which need to be studied concretely. Thus it is to be noted that the mass of the peasants, although they carry out an essential function in the world of production, do not elaborate their own "organic" intellectuals, and do not "assimilate" any class of traditional intellectuals, although other social groups take many of their intellectuals from the peasant masses, and a great many of the traditional intellectuals are of peasant origin.

(2) But every "essential" social class emerging into history from the preceding economic structure, and as an expression of one of the developments of this structure, has found, at least in all history up till now, intellectual categories which were pre-existing and which, moreover, appeared as representatives of an historical continuity uninterrupted even by the most complicated and radical changes in social and political forms.

The most typical of these intellectual categories is that of the ecclesiastics, monopolisers for a long time (for a complete historical phase which is partly characterised by this monopoly) of certain important services: namely, the religious ideology, the philosophy, and the science of the era, together with the school, education, morality, justice, charity, assistance, etc. The category of the ecclesiastics can be considered as the intellectual category organically tied to the landed aristocracy: legally it was on a level with the aristocracy, with whom it shared the exercise of feudal landownership and the enjoyment of the State privileges bound up with property.[1] But the monopoly

[1] For one category of these intellectuals, perhaps the most important after the "ecclesiastical"—for the prestige and the social function exercised in primitive societies—the category of *doctors* in a broad sense, that is, if all those who "battle" or appear to battle against death and sickness—it will be necessary to compare Arturo Castiglioni's *History of Medicine*. Remember that there has been and in certain areas continues to be a connection between religion and medicine: hospitals in the hands of monks for certain organisational functions, in addition to the fact that when the doctor appears the priest appears (exorcisms, various forms of attendance, etc.)—Many great religious figures were also or were conceived of as great "healers"; the idea of the miracle up to the resurrection of the dead. For kings also the belief lasted for a long time that they cured by laying on their hands, etc.

of the superstructure on the part of the ecclesiastics[1] was not exercised without struggles and limitations, and so we see the birth, in various forms (to be studied and researched into concretely) of other categories favoured and enlarged by the strengthening of the centralised power of the monarchy to the point of absolutism. Thus the aristocracy of the robe came to be formed, with its own privileges, a class of administrators, etc.; scientists, theoreticians, non-ecclesiastical philosophers, etc.

Just as these various categories of traditional intellectuals have a sense of their own uninterrupted historical continuity, of their "qualifications" and of *esprit de corps*, so they see themselves as autonomous and independent of the ruling social group. This view of themselves is not without consequences in the ideological and political field, consequences of vast importance: the whole of idealist philosophy can easily be connected with this assumed position of the social complex of intellectuals, and may be defined as the expression of this social utopia through which intellectuals believe themselves to be "independent", autonomous, clothed in their own characters, etc.

But if the Pope and the upper hierarchy of the Church believe that they are more tied to Christ and the Apostles than they are to Senators Agnelli and Benni, the same is not true of Gentile and Croce, for example; Croce especially feels himself strongly tied to Aristotle and Plato, but he does not conceal that he is tied to Senators Agnelli and Benni, and it is precisely in this fact that the most significant characteristic of Croce's philosophy is to be sought.

What are the "maximum" limits for the connotation of the word "intellectual"? Can a unitary criterion be found for characterising equally all the many varied intellectual activities and for distinguishing these at the same time and in an essential way from the activities of other social groupings? The most widespread methodological error seems to be that of looking for this distinguishing criterion within the sphere of intellectual activities, rather than examining the whole general complex of social relations within which these activities (and hence the groups which personify them) are to be found. Indeed, the worker or

[1] From this arises the general use of "intellectual" or "specialist", of the word "clerk" in many languages of neo-Latin origin or which were influenced strongly, through the Church, by neo-Latin languages, with its correlative of "lay" in the sense of profane, non-specialist.

the proletarian, for example, are not specifically characterised by their manual or skilled work, but by this work performed in certain conditions and in certain social relations. And it has already been observed that the capitalist, through his very function, must to a certain extent possess a certain number of qualifications of an intellectual kind, although his social position is not determined by these but precisely by those general relations which determine the position of the capitalist in industry.

All men are intellectuals, one could therefore say; but all men do not have the function of intellectuals in society.[1]

When we distinguish intellectuals and non-intellectuals we are in fact referring only to the immediate social function of the category of professional intellectuals, that is to say, we are taking account of the direction in which the greater part of the specific professional activity, whether in intellectual elaboration or in muscular-nervous effort, throws its weight. This means that, if we can speak of intellectuals, we cannot speak of non-intellectuals, because non-intellectuals do not exist. But the relationship itself between an effort of intellectual-cerebral elaboration and muscular-nervous effort is not always the same; therefore we have different levels of specific intellectual activity. There is no human activity from which all intellectual intervention can be excluded—*homo faber* cannot be separated from *homo sapiens*. Finally, every man, outside his own job, develops some intellectual activity; he is, in other words, a "philosopher", an artist, a man of taste, he shares a conception of the world, he has a conscious line of moral conduct, and so contributes towards maintaining or changing a conception of the world, that is, towards encouraging new modes of thought.

The problem of creating a new class of intellectuals consists, therefore, in the critical elaboration of the intellectual activity which exists at a certain stage of development in everyone, changing its relation with the muscular-nervous effort towards a new equilibrium and assuring that the muscular-nervous effort itself, in so far as it is a general practical activity which is perpetually changing the physical and social world, shall become the foundation of a new and integral conception of the

---

[1] Thus, since anyone at any time can fry a couple of eggs or mend a hole in a jacket, we do not say that everyone is a cook or a tailor.

world. The popularised traditional type of intellectual is represented by the literary man, the philosopher, the artist. Because of this, journalists, who regard themselves as literary men, philosophers and artists, regard themselves also as the "true" intellectuals. In the modern world technical education, strictly tied to even the most primitive and unqualified industrial work, must form the basis for the new type of intellectual.

It is on this basis that *Ordine Nuovo* worked, week by week, to develop certain forms of new intellectualism and to determine its new concepts, and this was not a minor reason for its success, because such a presentation corresponded to latent aspirations and conformed to actual forms of life. The mode of existence of the new intellectual can no longer consist of eloquence, the external and momentary arousing of sentiments and passions, but must consist of being actively involved in practical life, as a builder, an organiser, "permanently persuasive" because he is not purely an orator—and nevertheless superior to the abstract mathematical spirit; from technique-labour he reaches technique-science and the humanist historical conception, without which he remains a "specialist" and does not become a "leader" (specialist plus politician).

Historically specialised categories are formed in this way for carrying out the intellectual function; they are formed in connection with all social classes but especially in connection with the most important social groups, and undergo more extensive and complex elaborations in connection with the ruling social class. One of the most important characteristics of every class which develops towards power is its struggle to assimilate and conquer "ideologically" the traditional intellectuals. Assimilations and conquests are the more rapid and effective the more the given social class puts forward simultaneously its own organic intellectuals.

The enormous development in scholastic activity and organisation (in the broad sense) in the societies which arose out of the mediæval world indicate what importance intellectual categories and functions assume in the modern world: how the effort has been made to deepen and widen the "intellectuality" of every individual, as well as to increase and refine specialisation. This results from the work of scholastic institutions of various levels right up to the organisations to promote so-called "high culture", in every sphere of learning and technique.

The schools are the instrument for producing intellectuals at various levels. The complexity of the intellectual function in different States can be measured by the number of specialised schools and their degree of division into hierarchies: the more extensive is the scholastic "area" and the more numerous the "vertical levels" of the schools, the more complex will be the cultural world, the civilisation of any State. We can find a simile in the sphere of industrial technique: the industrialisation of a country is measured by its equipment for constructing machines and the manufacture of ever more accurate instruments to construct machines and tools for constructing machines, etc. The country which is best equipped for making instruments for experimental laboratories and for making instruments to test those instruments, can be called the most advanced in the technico-industrial field, the most civilised, etc. It is the same in the training of intellectuals and in the schools devoted to this; schools and institutions of high culture are alike in this. Even in this field, quantity cannot be divorced from quality. The most refined technico-cultural specialisation requires the greatest possible extension of primary education and the greatest care to encourage secondary education for the largest number. Naturally, this need for creating the broadest possible basis for the selection and training of people with the highest technical qualifications—of giving, that is, a democratic structure to high culture and advanced technique—has its inconveniences: the possibility is created of large unemployment crises among the middle intellectual strata, as in fact happens in all modern societies.

It should be noted that in reality the elaboration of intellectual groups does not take place on an abstract democratic basis, but according to very concrete traditional historical processes. Classes have been formed which traditionally "produce" intellectuals, and these are the same as those who are commonly noted for "thrift", i.e. the rural petty and middle bourgeoisie, and the same strata of the petty and middle bourgeoisie in the cities. The different distribution of different types of school (classical and professional) in the "economic" field and the different aspirations of the various categories of these classes determine or give shape to the production of different branches of intellectual specialisation. Thus in Italy the rural bourgeoisie produces especially state officials and free professionals, whereas the city bourgeoisie produces technicians for industry; and therefore Northern Italy produces especially technicians and Southern Italy especially officials and professional people.

The relationship between intellectuals and the world of production is not immediate, as is the case for fundamental social groups; it is "mediated", in different levels, by the whole social fabric, and by the complex of the superstructure of which the intellectuals are in fact the "officials". One could measure the "organic position" of the different intellectual strata, their more or less close connection with a fundamental social class, fixing a gradation of functions and of the superstructure from bottom to top (from the structural base upwards). For the moment we can fix two great "floors" of the superstructure: that which can be called "civil society", i.e. all the organisations which are commonly called "private", and that of "political society or the State", which corresponds to the function of "hegemony" which the ruling class exercises over the whole of society and to that of "direct rule" or of command which is expressed in the State and in "juridical" government. Intellectuals are the "officers" of the ruling class for the exercise of the subordinate functions of social hegemony and political government, i.e. (1) of the "spontaneous" consent given by the great masses of the population to the direction imprinted on social life by the fundamental ruling class, a consent which comes into existence "historically" from the "prestige" (and hence from the trust) accruing to the ruling class from its position and its function in the world of production; (2) of the apparatus of State coercion, which "legally" ensures the discipline of those groups which do not "consent" either actively or passively, but is constituted for the whole of society in anticipation of moments of crisis in command and direction when spontaneous consent diminishes.

This statement of the problem has the effect of greatly broadening the concept of intellectual, but only in this way is it possible to reach a concrete approximation to reality. This way of presenting the question strikes a blow against preconceptions of caste: it is true that the very function of organising social hegemony and State rule gives rise to a certain division of labour and so to a certain gradation of qualifications, in some of which no leading or organising attribute any longer appears: in the apparatus of social and State leadership there exists a whole series of jobs of a manual and instrumental character (of rule and not of concept, of agent and not of official or functionary, etc.); but evidently this distinction needs to be made, as it will also be necessary to make others. In fact intellectual activity must be divided into levels from an intrinsic point of view as well, levels which in moments of extreme opposition offer a true qualitative difference: in the highest grade will have to be placed the creators of the various sciences, of philosophy, art, etc.; in the lowest, the most humble "administrators" and propagators of already existing traditional and accumulated intellectual riches.[1]

In the modern world the category of the intellectuals, understood in this way, has been inordinately enlarged. They have been produced in imposing numbers by the democratico-bureaucratic social system, beyond what is justified by the social needs of production, even if justified by the political needs of the fundamental ruling class. Hence Loria's conception of the unproductive "worker" (but unproductive with reference to whom and to what mode of production?), which may be partly justified if one takes account of the fact that these masses exploit their position to assign themselves huge cuts out of the national income. The mass formation has standardised individuals in terms of both individual and psychological peculiarities, resulting in the same phenomena which exists in all other standardised masses: competition, which provides the need for professional defensive organisations, unemployment, scholastic overproduction, emigration, etc.

[1] Military organisation, in this case also, provides a model for these complex gradations: subordinate officers, superior officers, General Staff; and there is no need to forget the N.C.O.'s whose real importance is greater than is usually thought. It is interesting to note that all these parts feel solidarity together, and moreover that the lower strata show a more apparent *esprit de corps* and derive from it an "arrogance" which provides the subject of many jokes.

# THE ORGANISATION OF EDUCATION AND CULTURE

IN modern civilisation all practical activities have, generally speaking, become so complex and learning so interwoven with life that every kind of practical activity tends to create a school for its own leaders and specialists, and hence to create a group of specialised intellectuals of a higher level to teach in these schools. Thus, alongside the older, traditional type of school which we may call "humanistic", and which was directed towards developing an as yet undifferentiated general culture in each human individual (the fundamental ability to think and guide oneself in life), there has been growing up a whole system of separate schools at various levels for whole professional branches or for already specialised and precisely differentiated professions. Moreover, today's widespread educational crisis can be precisely linked to the fact that this process of differentiation and specialisation has taken place chaotically, without clear and precise principles, without a well thought out and consciously fixed plan. The crisis in educational programmes and organisation, that is, of the general direction of a policy for developing modern intellectual cadres, is to a large extent an aspect and a complication of a more comprehensive and general organic crisis.

The basic division of schools into classical (i.e. grammar) and trade schools was a rational scheme: trade schools for the instrumental classes, classical schools for the ruling classes and intellectuals. The development of the industrial base in both town and country led to a growing need for a new type of urban intellectual: alongside the classical school there developed the technical school (professional but not manual), and this brought into question the very principle of the concrete orientation of general culture, of the humanist orientation of general culture based on the Greco-Roman tradition. This orientation, once brought into question was in fact doomed, since its formative capacity was largely based on the general and traditionally indisputable prestige of a particular form of civilisation.

Today the tendency is to abolish every kind of "disinterested" (not immediately interested) and "formative" school and to leave only a reduced number of them for a tiny *élite* of ladies and gentlemen who do not have to think of preparing themselves for a professional future, and to spread ever more widely the specialised professional schools in which the destiny of the pupil and his future activity are predetermined. The crisis will find a solution which rationally should follow these lines: a single humanistic, formative primary school of general culture which will correctly balance the development of ability for manual (technical, industrial) work with the development of ability for intellectual work. From this type of single school, following repeated tests for professional aptitude, the pupil will pass either into one of the specialised schools or into productive work.

Attention must be paid to the growing tendency by which every kind of practical activity creates its own specialised school, just as every kind of intellectual activity tends to create its own cultural circles, which acquire the function of post-scholastic institutions specialised in organising the conditions under which it may be possible to keep up to date with progress in their own branch of science.

Deliberating bodies are tending more and more to distinguish two "organic" aspects of their activity—the purely deliberative which is their essential function, and the technico-cultural by which questions requiring solution are first examined by experts and scientifically analysed. This latter activity has already created a whole bureacratic body with a new structure, since in addition to the offices of professional experts who prepare technical material for the deliberating bodies, there has been created a second body of more or less "voluntary" and disinterested functionaries chosen from time to time from industry, the banks, finance. This is one of the mechanisms by which the career bureaucracy has ended by controlling democratic and parliamentary régimes; now the mechanism is extending itself organically and absorbing into its own circle the leading specialists of private practical activity which thus controls both régimes and bureaucracies. Since this is a question of a necessary organic development which tends to integrate the personnel specialised in political technique with the personnel specialised in concrete questions of the administration of practical activities essential to large complex modern national societies, all attempts to exorcise this tendency from outside only result in moralising sermons and rhetorical moans.

The question arises of modifying the training of the technical political personnel, integrating its culture according to new necessities, and of developing new types of specilised functionaries who shall integrate their deliberating activities in a collegiate way. The traditional type of political "ruler", trained only for formal-legal activities, is becoming an anachronism and represents a danger to State life: the ruler must possess that minimum of general technical culture to enable him, if not to "create" the correct solution autonomously, at least to judge between the solutions put forward by the experts and to select the correct one from the "synthetic" viewpoint of political technique.

One type of deliberating college which seeks to incorporate the necessary technical competence to work realistically has been described elsewhere,[1] where I spoke of what happens on the editorial boards of certain reviews, which function as cultural circles at the same time as editorial boards. The circle criticises in a collegiate way and so contributes towards developing the work of individual members of the editorial staff, whose own task is organised according to a rationally worked out plan and division of labour.

Through discussions and joint criticism (consisting of suggestions, advice, indications of method, constructive criticism directed towards mutual learning), by which each man functions as a specialist in his own subject to improve the collective competence, the average level of each individual is raised. It reaches the height or the capacity of the best trained and assures the review not only of ever better selected and organic contributions but creates the conditions for the rise of a homogeneous group of intellectuals trained to produce regular and methodical "literary" activity (not only in *livres d'occasion* and partial studies, but in organic general works as well).

Undoubtedly in this kind of collective activity each job produces the capacity and possibility for new work, since it creates ever more organic conditions of work: card indexes, bibliographical notes, collections of basic specialised works, etc. A rigorous struggle is required against habits of dilettantism, improvisation, "oratorical" and declamatory solutions. It is important for reports, and this applies to

[1] Not included in this selection.—*Trans.*

criticisms, to be made in written form, in short succinct notes. This can be ensured by distributing material in good time, etc. Writing notes and criticisms is a didactic principle rendered necessary by the need to combat habits of prolixity, declamation and sophistry created by oratory. . . .

An important point in the study of the practical organisation of the unitary school concerns the various levels of the scholastic career corresponding to the age and intellectual-moral development of the pupil and the ends which the school itself wants to achieve. The unitary, humanistic school (humanist in the broad sense and not only in the traditional meaning), or school of general culture, should set out to introduce young people to social activity after having brought them to a certain level of maturity and ability, of intellectual and practical creation, independent in orientation and initiative. The fixing of the leaving age depends on general economic conditions, since these may impose a certain immediate demand for productive ability. The unitary school requires that the State should take over the expenses of maintaining the scholars which today fall on the family. It transforms the budget of the education department from top to bottom, extending and elaborating it in unparalleled ways. The whole task of educating and forming the younger generation becomes public instead of private, since only in this way can it involve the whole generation without distinctions of group or caste. But this transformation of scholastic activity requires an unparalleled enlarging of the practical organisation of the schools, i.e. of the buildings, scientific equipment, teaching staff, etc. The teaching staff especially must be increased, because the efficiency of the school is the greater the closer the relationship between teacher and pupil—a fact which raises other problems which cannot be solved easily or quickly. The question of school buildings is also not a simple one, because this type of school ought to be a school-college (boarding school), with dormitories, dining-rooms, specialised libraries, rooms suited for seminar work, etc. Therefore, to begin with, the new type of school must and can only be open to restricted groups of young people selected by competition or nominated by suitable institutions.

The unitary school should correspond to the period represented by the elementary and middle school (i.e. 7 to 15—*Trans.*), but reorganised not only in teaching content and method, but also in the arrangement of the various stages of the school career. The elementary grade should not be more than three-four years, and together with the teaching of the first "instrumental" notions of education—reading, writing, arithmetic, geography, history—special attention must be paid to a side which is ignored today—"rights and duties", i.e. the first notions of State and Society as basic elements of a new conception of the world which conflicts with ideas derived from different traditional social environments, ideas which belong to what may be termed folk-lore. The teaching problem to be solved is that of tempering and fertilising the dogmatic methods, which cannot be dispensed with in this age group. The remainder of the course should not last more than six years, so that at fifteen to sixteen years the child should have completed all the grades of the unitary school.

The objection may be made that such a course is too difficult, because too rapid, if one wants effectively to attain the results that the present day organisation of the classical school sets before itself but does not reach. But it can be said that the conditions under which the new organisation must function will include factors which will make the course in fact too slow for at least a part of the pupils. What are these factors? In a number of families, especially those of the intellectual strata, the children get some training at home, an extension and inte-gration of school life; they absorb, so to speak, from the "atmosphere" a whole number of notions and attitudes which make their school career proper a good deal easier. They already possess and may develop further an awareness of literary language, i.e. a means of expression and awareness technically superior to the means possessed by the average child between the ages of six and twelve. Thus town pupils simply through living in towns have already absorbed, even before they are six, a number of ideas and attitudes which make their school career easier, quicker, more useful. The internal life of the unitary school must offer the basis at least for these factors to take effect, in addition to the fact that presumably a whole network of nursery schools and other institutions will be developed parallel to the unitary school where, even before school age, the young children will acquire pre-schooling notions and attitudes. In fact the unitary school should be organised like a college with a twenty-four hour collective life, free from present-day forms of hypocritical and mechanical discipline. Studies should be conducted collectively with help from the masters and best pupils, even in the hours of so-called private study, etc.

The basic problem arises in that phase which in the present day school career is represented by the *liceo* (fifteen to eighteen years). So far as the kind of teaching goes, this is today in no way different from the earlier school, apart from the abstract assumption of the pupil's greater intellectual and moral maturity, corresponding to his being older and more experienced.

In fact today from *liceo* to university, or from school proper to life, there is a jump, a real break in continuity, not a rational transition from quantity (age) to quality (intellectual and moral maturity). From almost purely dogmatic teaching, in which memory plays a large part, one moves on to the creative phase of independent work; from school with its imposed and authoritatively controlled study discipline one moves on to a phase of study or professional work where intellectual self-discipline and moral independence are theoretically unlimited. And this happens immediately after the crisis of puberty, when the flame of instinctive and elementary passions has not yet stopped struggling against the checks of a character and moral conscience still in formation.

It is just this final phase of the unitary school which must be conceived and organised as the decisive stage in which one is trying to create the fundamental values of "humanism", intellectual self-discipline and moral independence, preparatory to later specialisation either of a scholarly (university study) or immediate practical-productive character (industry, bureaucracy, trade organisation, etc.) The study and learning of creative methods in science and life must begin in this last stage at school and no longer be the monopoly of the universities or be left to chance in everyday life; this stage at school must already help to develop the elements of independent responsibility in individuals. It must be a creative school. But the distinction must be made between creative and active schools even in the form given by the Dalton method. The whole of the unitary school is an active school, though limits must be placed on anarchistic ideologies in this field and energy be devoted to vindicating the duties of adults, i.e. of the State, to make the new generations "conform". The active school is still in its romantic stage, where the arguments used to attack mechanical and

Jesuitical kinds of education are being extended fanatically for purposes of opposition and polemic. It must now enter its "classical", rational phase. It must seek in the ends to be achieved the natural source for developing its forms and methods.

The creative school is the consummation of the active school. In its first stage it tends towards discipline, and hence towards levelling, so as to obtain some kind of "conformity" which could be called "dynamic"; in its creative stage, on the basis of the "collectivisation" of the social type, it seeks to expand the personality which has become independent and responsible but with a solid social and homogeneous moral conscience. Thus, the creative school does not mean a school of "inventors and discoverers"; it means a stage and method of research and knowledge, not a predetermined programme with the obligation of originality and innovation at all costs. It means that learning takes place mainly through a spontaneous and independent effort by the student, in which the teacher only acts as a friendly guide, as happens or ought to happen in the universities. Discovery of a truth by oneself without suggestion or outside help is creation, even though the truth is an old one. It shows mastery of the method; it indicates that one has entered a phase of intellectual maturity where it is possible to discover new truths. Therefore in this phase the basic scholastic activities will take place in seminars, libraries, laboratories. The necessary information will be gathered for orientation in a profession.

The advent of the unitary school marks the beginning of new relations between intellectual and industrial work, not only in school but in the whole of social life. The unitary principle will therefore be reflected in all organs of culture, transforming them and giving them a new content.

*Part Three*

*THE MODERN PRINCE*

# THE MODERN PRINCE
## Essays on the Science of Politics in the Modern Age

*Notes on Machiavelli's Politics*

THE fundamental characteristic of *The Prince* is that it is not a systematic treatment, but a "living" book, in which political ideology and political science are fused in the dramatic form of a "myth". In contrast to the utopia and the scholastic tract, the forms in which political science was expressed before Machiavelli, this treatment has given his conception the form of fantasy and art, by it the doctrinal and rational element is embodied in the person of a *condottiere*, representing plastically and "anthropomorphically" the symbol of the "collective will". The process of formation of a determined collective will, for a determined political end, is here represented not through disquisitions and pedantic classifications of the principles and criteria of a mode of action, but through the qualities, characteristic traits, duties, necessities of a concrete person, which excite the artistic fantasy of those he wants to convince and give a more concrete form to political passions.[1]

*The Prince* of Machiavelli could be studied as an historical example of the Sorellian "myth", that is, of a political ideology which is not presented as a cold utopia or as a rational doctrine, but as a creation of concrete fantasy which works on a dispersed and pulverised people in order to arouse and organise their collective will. The utopian characteristic of *The Prince* lies in the fact that the Prince did not exist in historical reality, did not present himself to the Italian people in a directly objective way, but was a purely doctrinaire abstraction, the symbol of a leader, the ideal *condottiere;* but the emotional, mythical elements contained throughout this small book, with very effective dramatic movement, are recapitulated and come to life in the conclusion, the invocation of a "really existing" prince. Throughout the book Machiavelli

---

[1] It will have to be seen whether any political writers before Machiavelli have presented their writings like *The Prince*. The close of the book is tied up also with this "mythical" characteristic: after having presented the ideal *condottiere*, Machiavelli, in a passage of great artistic effect, calls on the real *condottiere* to bring him to life historically: this impassioned plea reflects on the whole book and confers on it precisely this dramatic character. In Luigi Russo's *Prolegomini*, Machiavelli is called the artist of politics, and once even the expression of "myth" occurs, but not in the precise sense shown above.

deals with what the Prince must be in order to lead the people towards the foundation of a new State, and the argument is conducted with rigorous logic, with scientific detachment; in the conclusion Machiavelli makes himself the people, merges himself with the people, not with the people in a "general" sense, but with the people whom Machiavelli has convinced with the preceding tract, whose conscious expression he becomes and feels himself to be, with whom he feels himself identified: it seems that the whole of the "logical" work is only a reflection of the people, an internal reasoning which takes place inside the popular consciousness and has its conclusions in an impassioned, urgent cry. Passion, from reasoning about itself, becomes "emotion", fever, fanaticism for action. That is why the epilogue of *The Prince* is not something extrinsic, "stuck on" from outside, rhetorical, but must be understood as a necessary part of the work, and, moreover, as that part which sheds a true light over the whole work and makes it seem like a "political manifesto".

We can study how Sorel did not advance from the conception of the ideology-myth to an understanding of the political party, but stopped short at the conception of the trade union. It is true that for Sorel the "myth" did not find its greatest expression in the union as an organisation of a collective will, but in the practical action of the union and of an already operating collective will, practical action whose greatest realisation was, according to him, the general strike, that is "passive activity", so to speak, of a negative and preliminary character (the positive character is provided only by the agreement reached by the associated wills), an activity which does not envisage its own "active and constructive" phase. In Sorel therefore two necessities were in conflict: that of the myth and that of criticism of the myth, since "every pre-established plan is utopian and reactionary". The solution was left to irrational impulse, to "chance" (in the Bergsonian sense of "vital impulse"), or to "spontaneity".

But can a myth be "non-constructive", can it be imagined, according to Sorel's intuitions, that an instrument is productive of an effect which leaves the collective will in the primitive and elementary phase of its mere formation, through distinction (through "splitting away"), even though with violence, that is, by destroying existing moral and legal relations? Will not this collective will, thus elementarily formed, immediately cease to exist, and be scattered in an infinity of single wills which for the positive phase follow different and contrasting directions? In addition there is the question that destruction, negation, cannot exist without an implicit construction, affirmation, and not in a "metaphysical" sense but in practice, i.e. politically, as a party programme. In this case we see that behind spontaneity is presupposed pure mechanicalism, behind freedom (vital will-drive) a maximum of determinism, behind idealism an absolute materialism.

The modern prince, the myth-prince, cannot be a real person, a concrete individual; it can only be an organism; a complex element of society in which the cementing of a collective will, recognised and partially asserted in action, has already begun. This organism is already provided by historical development and it is the political party: the first cell containing the germs of collective will which are striving to become universal and total. In the modern world only an immediate and imminent historico-political action, characterised by the necessity for rapid and lightning movement, can be mythically embodied in a concrete individual; this rapidity can only be rendered necessary by a great imminent danger, a great danger which in fact brings about simultaneously the enflaming of passions and fanaticism, abolishing critical sense and the corroding irony which can destroy the "divine" character of a *condottiere* (which is what happened in the Boulanger adventure.) But an immediate action of this kind, by its very nature, cannot be long drawn out or have an organic character. It will almost always be of the restoration and reorganisation type and not of the type proper to the foundation of new States and new national and social structures (as was the case in Machiavelli's *Prince*, in which the aspect of restoration was only theoretical, that is, bound up with the literary concept of an Italy descending from Rome which must restore the order and power of Rome).[1] It will have a "defensive"

---

[1] In addition to the examples offered by the great absolute monarchies of France and Spain, Machiavelli was inspired to his conception of the *necessity* of a unitary Italian State by the memory of Rome. It must be shown, however, that Machiavelli is not on this account to be confused with the literary-rhetorical tradition. Especially because this element is not exclusive and not even predominant, and the necessity for a great national State is not deduced from it, and also because even the reference to Rome is less abstract than it appears, if it is placed correctly in the climate of Humanism and the Renaissance. In Book VII of *The Art of War* we read; "This province (Italy) seems born for the reviving of dead things, as we have seen with poetry, painting and sculpture; why should it not therefore rediscover military virtue?" etc. His remarks of this kind will have to be grouped together to establish their exact character.

and not an originally creative character, in which, that is, it is presupposed that there is an already existing collective will which is enervated, dispersed, which has suffered a dangerous and threatening but not decisive and catastrophic collapse, and which it is necessary to reconcentrate and strengthen and not that a collective will is to be created *ex novo*, originally, and to be directed towards very concrete and rational ends, but ends whose concreteness and rationality have not yet been verified and criticised by any effective and universally known historical experience.

The "abstract" character of Sorel's conception of the "myth" is apparent from his aversion (which takes the emotional form of ethical repugnance) for the Jacobins, who were certainly a "categoric incarnation" of Machiavelli's Prince. *The Modern Prince* must contain a part dedicated to Jacobinism (in the integral significance which this notion has had historically and ought to have conceptually), as an example of how a collective will was formed and operated concretely, which in at least some of its aspects was an original creation, *ex novo*. It is necessary to define collective will and political will in general in the modern sense; will as working consciousness of historical necessity, as protagonist of a real and effective historical drama.

One of the first parts ought in fact to be dedicated to the "collective will", posing the question in this way: "When can the conditions for the arousing and development of a national-popular collective will be said to exist?" Hence an historical (economic) analysis must be made of the social structure of the given country together with a "dramatic" presentation of the attempts made throughout the centuries to arouse this will and the reasons for the successive failures. Why was there no absolute monarchy in Italy at the time of Machiavelli? One must go back to the end of the Roman Empire (questions of language, the intellectuals, etc.) in order to understand the function of the mediæval Communes, the significance of Catholicism, etc.: it is necessary, in fact, to make a sketch of the whole of Italian history, synthetic but exact.

The reason for the successive failures of the attempts to create a national-popular collective will is to be sought in the existence of certain social groups, which were formed by the dissolution of the Communal bourgeoisie, and in the particular character of other groups which reflect the international function of Italy as the seat of the Church and depositary of the Holy Roman Empire, etc. This function and the consequent position led to an internal situation which can be called "economico-corporative", that is, politically, the worst of the forms of feudal society, the least progressive and the most stagnant: there was always lacking, and could not be constituted, an efficient Jacobin force, just such a force which in other nations awakened and organised the national popular collective will and founded the modern States. Do the conditions for this will finally exist, or what is the present relationship between these conditions and the forces opposed to them? Traditionally the opposing forces have been the landed aristocracy and more generally landed property in all its forms, with its characteristic Italian trait which is a special "rural bourgeoisie", heir of the parasitism bequeathed to modern times by the ruin, as a class, of the Communal bourgeoisie (the hundred cities, the cities of silence). The positive conditions are to be sought in the existence of urban social groups, conveniently developed in the field of industrial production, who have reached a certain level of historico-political culture. Any formation of a national-popular collective will is impossible, unless the great mass of peasant cultivators breaks *simultaneously* into political life. Machiavelli understood this by his reform of the militia, which is what the Jacobins did in the French Revolution, and in this understanding we can see the precocious Jacobinism of Machiavelli, the germ (more or less fertile) of his conception of the national revolution. All history since 1815 shows the efforts of the traditional classes to prevent the formation of a collective will of this kind, to maintain their "economico-corporative" power in an international system of passive equilibrium.

An important part of the modern Prince will have to be devoted to the question of intellectual and moral reform, that is, to the question of religion or world outlook. In this field also we find a traditional absence of Jacobinism and fear of Jacobinism (the latest philosophical expression of which fear is the Malthusian standpoint of B. Croce towards religion). The Modern Prince must and cannot but be the preacher and organiser of intellectual and moral reform, which means creating the basis for a later development of the national popular collective will towards the realisation of a higher and total form of modern civilisation.

These two fundamental points—the formation of a national-popular collective will of which the modern Prince is at the same time the organiser and active working expression, and a moral and intellectual reform—should constitute the structure of the work. The concrete points of programme must be incorporated in the first part, i.e. they should result "dramatically" from the discourse and not be a cold and pedantically reasoned exposition.

Can there be a cultural reform and an uplifting of the civilisation of the depressed strata of society without there first being an economic reform and a change in their social position and place in the economic world? Intellectual and moral reform must be tied to a programme of economic reform; moreover, the programme of economic reform is precisely the concrete way in which every intellectual and moral reform is presented. The Modern Prince, in developing itself, changes the system of intellectual and moral relations, since its development means precisely that every act is conceived as useful or harmful, as virtuous or wicked, only in so far as it has the Modern Prince itself as a point of reference and helps to increase its power or oppose it. The Prince takes the place, in the conscience, of the divinity or of the categorical imperative, and becomes the basis of a modern laicism, of a complete laicisation of the whole of life and of all customary relations.

## The Science of Politics

The fundamental innovation introduced by Marxism into the science of politics and history is the proof that there does not exist an abstract, fixed and immutable "human nature" (a concept which certainly derives from religious thought and transcendentalism); but that human nature is the totality of historically determined social relations, that is, an historical fact, ascertainable, within certain limits, by the methods of philology and criticism. Therefore, political science must be conceived in its concrete content (and also in its logical formulation) as an organism in development. It should be observed, however, that the direction given by Machiavelli to the question of politics (that is, the assertion implicit in his writings that politics is an independent activity, with its own principles and laws distinct from those of morality and religion, a proposition of great philosophical importance, since it implicitly originates a conception of morality and religion, i.e. it began a whole conception of the world) is still discussed and contradicted today, and has not succeded in becoming "common sense". What does this mean? Does it only mean that the intellectual and moral revolution whose elements are contained *in nuce* in Machiavelli's thought has not yet come about, has not yet become a public and manifest form of the national culture? Or is it merely of present-day political significance, serving to show the gap that exists between rulers and ruled, that two cultures exist—one of the rulers and one of the ruled—and that the ruling class, like the Church, has its own attitude towards the simple folk dictated by the necessity on the one hand of not separating itself from them, and, on the other, of keeping them convinced that Machiavelli is nothing but a diabolical apparition?

In this way the problem is posed of the significance Machiavelli had in his own times and of the ends which he set himself in his books, and especially in *The Prince*. Machiavelli's doctrine was not in his own time purely "bookish", a monopoly of isolated thinkers, a secret book which circulated among the initiated. Machiavelli's style is not that of a systematic writer of tracts, as was usual in both the Middle Ages and Humanism. On the contrary, it is the style of a man of action, a man who wants to encourage action, it is the style of a party "manifesto". The "moralistic" interpretation given by Foscolo is certainly wrong; still, is it true that Machiavelli has *unveiled* something and not only theorised reality: but to what end? A moralistic or a political end? It is usually said that Machiavelli's standards for political behaviour "are applied but not spoken about"; the great politicians—it is said— begin by cursing Machiavelli, declaring themselves anti-Machiavellians, just in order to apply his standards "sanctimoniously". Would not Machiavelli in this case have been un-Machiavellian, one of those who "know the tricks of the game" and stupidly teach them to others, whereas popular Machiavellianism teaches the opposite? Croce's assertion that, as Machiavellianism is a science, it can serve reactionaries as well as democrats, as the art of fencing helps both gentlemen and brigands, to defend themselves and to murder, and that Foscolo's judgment should be understood in this sense, is true abstractly. Machiavelli himself notes that the things he is writing are applied, and have always been applied by the greatest men in history; it does not seem, therefore, that he wants to advise those who already know; his style is not that of disinterested scientific activity, nor can he be thought to have arrived at this theses of political science along the path of philosophical speculation, which in this particular subject would have been something of a miracle in his time, if even today it finds so much contradiction and opposition.

We can therefore suppose that Machiavelli had in view "those who do not know", that he intended to give political education to "those who do not know", not a negative political education of hatred for tyrants, as Foscolo seems to mean, but a positive education of those who must recognise certain necessary means, even if those of tyrants, because they want certain ends. The man who is born into the tradition of government through the whole complex of his education which he absorbs from his family environment, in which dynastic and patrimonial interests predominate, acquires almost automatically the characteristics of the realistic politician. Who then "does not know"? The revolutionary class of the time, the Italian "people" and "nation", the citizen democracy which gave birth to Savonarola and Piero Soderini and not Castruccio and Valentino. It can be considered that Machiavelli wanted to persuade these forces of the necessity for a "leader", who would know what he wanted and how to obtain it and to accept him with enthusiasm even if his actions might be or appear to be contrary to the widely held ideology of the time, religion. This position of Machiavelli is repeated for Marxism. The necessity is repeated of being "anti-Machiavellian", of developing a theory and technique of politics which can help both sides in the struggle, but which it is thought will end by helping especially the side "which did not know", because in this side is held to exist the progressive force of history. In fact one result is achieved immediately: that of breaking up the unity based on traditional ideology, without which the new force would be unable to gain awareness of its own independent personality. Machiavellianism has helped to improve the traditional political technique of the conservative ruling groups, just as has Marxism; but this must not conceal its essentially revolutionary character, which is felt even today and which explains the whole of anti-Machiavellianism from that of the Jesuits to that of the pietistic Pasquale Villari.

## Elements of Politics

It really needs to be said that the first things to be forgotten are just the first points, the most elementary things; on the other hand if these are repeated incessantly they become the pillars of politics and of all collective action.

The first point is that there do in fact exist rulers and ruled, leaders and led. The whole of the science and art of politics is based on this primordial, irreducible (in certain general conditions) fact. The origin of this fact is a problem on its own which will have to be studied separately (at least, it can and will have to be studied how to minimise the fact and make it disappear, changing certain conditions identifiable as operating in this sense), but the fact remains that there do exist rulers and ruled, leaders and led. Given this fact it will have to be seen how one can rule in the most effective way (given certain ends), and how therefore to prepare the rulers in the best way (and the first section of the science and art of politics consists more precisely in this), and how, on the other hand, to know the lines of least resistance or the rational lines for gaining the obedience of the ruled and the led.

In the formation of leaders the premise is fundamental: does one wish there always to be rulers and ruled, or does one wish to create the conditions where the necessity for the existence of this division disappears? In other words, does one start from the premise of the perpetual division of the human race or does one believe that this is only an historical fact, answering to certain conditions? Nevertheless, it needs to be understood that the division of rulers and ruled, though in the last analysis it goes back to divisions between social groups, does in fact exist, given things as they are, even inside the bosom of each separate group, even a socially homogeneous one. In a sense it can be said that this division is a product of the division of labour, that it is a technical fact. Those people who see in everything only "technique", "technical" necessity, etc., speculate about this coexistence of motives so as to escape the fundamental problem.

Given that even inside the same group there exists a division between rulers and ruled, it is necessary to settle some immutable principles, and it is mainly on this question that the most serious "errors" come about, those which show themselves in the most criminal incapacity and are most difficult to correct. It is believed that when the principle of the group is laid down obedience ought to be automatic, should come about without the need to show its "necessity" and rationality, or even that it is beyond discussion (some people think, and what is worse, act on the thought, that obedience "will come" without being asked, without the paths being shown). So it is difficult to rid the leaders of dictatorial habits, that is, the conviction that something will be done because the leader thinks it is correct and rational that it should be done: if it is not done, the "blame" is put on those who "ought to have ", etc. So it is difficult to extirpate the criminal habit of neglecting to avoid useless sacrifices. Still, common sense shows that the greater number of collective (political) disasters come about because no attempt was made to avoid useless sacrifices, or no account was taken of the sacrifices of others and other people's skins were gambled with. Everyone has heard stories from officers at the front of how soldiers would readily risk their lives if it was necessary, but who would rebel when they saw themselves neglected. For example, a company was capable of going without food for many days when it saw that supplies could not get through because of *force majeur*, but it mutinied when one meal was skipped through neglect and bureaucracy, etc.

This principle is extended to all actions which demand sacrifice. Therefore, after every defeat, it is always necessary to look into the responsibility of the leaders, and this in a strict sense (for example: a front is made up of many sections and every section has its own leaders: it is possible that the leaders of one section may be more responsible for the defeat than those of another, but the question is one of degree and never of anyone's freedom from responsibility.)

Having laid down the principle that there exist leaders and led, rulers and ruled, it is true that up till now the "parties" have been the most appropriate method for producing leaders and the capacity for leadership ("parties" can present themselves under different names, even that of anti-party or of "negation of parties"; in reality even the so-called "independents" are party men, except that they would like to be "party leaders" through the grace of God and the imbecility of those who follow them).

Development of the general concept contained in the expression "public spirit". This expression has a very precise, historically determined significance. But this is the problem: does there exist something similar to what is called "public spirit" in every serious movement, i.e. one which is not the arbitrary expression of individualism, but is more or less justified? At the same time, "public spirit" presupposes "continuity", whether with the past, or rather with tradition, or with the future, i.e. which presupposes that every act is a stage in a complex process which has already begun and which will continue. The responsibility for this process, for being actors in this process, for being in solidarity with forces which are materially "unknown" but which are felt to be actively operating and are taken account of as though they were "material" and bodily present, is called in certain cases precisely "public spirit". It is evident that this awareness of "duration" must be concrete and not abstract, that is, in a certain sense, it must not pass certain limits. I assume that the smallest limits are one generation before and one generation after, which is no little time, since generations are counted not thirty years ahead and thirty years back but in an organic, historical way, which for the past at least is easy to understand. We feel solidarity with men who are today very old and who for us represent the "past" which still lives among us, which we need to know, of which we need to take account, which is one of the elements of the present and one of the premises for the future. And we feel solidarity with babies, with the newly born and growing generation for which we are responsible. (The "cult" of "tradition", which has a tendentious value, is something different, it implies a choice and a definite purpose, that is, it is at the basis of an ideology.) Still, if it can be said that "public spirit" in this sense exists in everything, we need time and again to fight against distortions of it and deviations from it.

"Action for the sake of action", struggle for the sake of struggle, etc. and especially shabby, petty individualism, which is a capricious satisfying of momentary impulses, etc. (In reality, the point is always that of Italian "apoliticism", which takes on these various picturesque and weird forms.) Individualism is only animal apoliticism, sectarianism is "apoliticism", and, if you look into it, sectarianism is a form of personal "patronage", whereas it lacks the party spirit which is the fundamental element of "public spirit". The proof that party spirit is the fundamental element of "public spirit" is one of the more conspicuous and most important to be sustained; *vice versa*, "individualism" is an animal element, "admired by foreigners", like the antics of the inhabitants of a zoo.

### The Political Party

I have said that the protagonist of the new Prince in modern times cannot be an individual hero, but the political party, that is, that particular party which, at different times and in the different internal relations of the various nations, aims (and is rationally and historically founded for this end) to found a new type of State.

It must be observed that in the totalitarian régimes, the traditional function of the institution of the Crown is in reality taken over by the party which is totalitarian precisely because it acquits this function. Although every party is the expression of a social group and only one social group, nevertheless certain parties represent only one social group, in certain given conditions, in so far as they exercise a function of balance and of arbitration between the interests of their own group and the other groups, and ensure that the development of the represented group takes place with the consent and assistance of the allied groups, if not actually of decidely opposed groups. The constitutional formula of the king or the president of a republic who "reigns but does not govern" is the juridical formula which expresses this function of arbiter, the concern of the constitutional parties not to "unmask" the Crown or the president; the formulæ of the non-responsibility of the head of the State for governmental acts and of ministerial responsibility, are the casuistry of the general principle of guardianship of the conception of State unity, of the consent of the governed for State action, whatever may be the immediate personnel and party of the government.

With the totalitarian party, these formulæ lose their meaning and the institutions which used to function according to such formulæ are diminished; but the function itself is incorporated in the party, which will exalt the abstract concept of "State" and will seek by various means to give the impression that the function of "impartial force" is active and effective.

Is political action (in the strict sense) necessary in order to be able to speak of a "political party"? It can be observed that in the modern world, in many countries, because of the needs of the struggle or for other causes, the organic and fundamental parties are split up into segments, each one of which assumes the name of "party" and even of an independent party. Often therefore the intellectual High Command of the organic party does not belong to any of these fractions but operates as a leading force standing on its own, above the parties and sometimes is even believed to be such by the public. This function can be studied with greater precision if we begin from the point of view that a newspaper (or a group of newspapers), a review (or group of reviews), is also a "party", or "fraction of a party", or "the function of a determined party". One could think of the function of *The Times* in England and of that which the *Corriere della Sera* had in Italy, and also of the function of the so-called "information Press", styling itself "apolitical", and even of the sporting and technical press. For the rest, the phenomenon offers interesting aspects in countries where a single governmental, totalitarian party exists: because such a party no longer has a strictly political function but only one of technique, propaganda, police, and of moral and cultural influence. The political influence is indirect: since, if no other legal parties exist, there always exist other parties either in fact or in tendency which are legally uncoercible, against which one polemicises and struggles as in a game of blindman's buff. In any case it is certain that in such parties the cultural functions predominate, giving rise to a political jargon: that is, political questions are reclothed in cultural forms and as such become unresolvable.

But one traditional party has an essentially "indirect" character, in other words, it presents itself explicitly as purely "educative" (*lucus*, etc.), moralistic, cultural (*sic*): and this is the anarchist movement: even so-called direct action (terrorism) is conceived as "propaganda" by example: from this the judgment may be further strengthened that the anarchist movement is not autonomous, but exists on the margin of the other parties, "to educate them". One can speak of an "anarchism" inherent in every organic party. (What are the "intellectual or cerebral anarchists" if not an aspect of this "marginalism" in respect of the great parties of the ruling social groups?) The "economist sect" itself was an historical aspect of this phenomenon.

Two forms of "party" that seem to abstain from immediate political action therefore present themselves: that constituted by an *élite* of men of culture, who have the function of leading from the point of view of culture, of general ideology, a large movement of allied parties (which are in reality fractions of the same organic party); and, in the most recent period, a party not of an *élite*, but of the masses, who as masses have no other political function than that of generic loyalty, of a military kind, to a visible or invisible political centre (often the visible centre is the mechanism of command of forces which are unwilling to show themselves in full light but only work indirectly, through interposed people and through an "interposed ideology"). The masses are simply for "manœuvring" and are "kept busy" with moral sermons, with sentimental goads, with messianic myths of an awaited fabulous age, in which all the present contradictions and poverty will be automatically resolved and healed.

To write the history of a political party, it is really necessary to face up to a whole series of problems, much less simple ones than Robert Michels, for example, believes, though he is held to be a specialist in the subject. What will the history of a party be? Will it be merely the account of the internal life of a political organisation? How it comes into existence, the first groups constituting it, the ideological polemics through which its programme and its conception of the world and of life were formed? In this case one would be dealing with the history of restricted intellectual groups and sometimes with the political biography of a single individual. The framework, therefore, will have to be larger and more comprehensive.

One will have to write the history of a certain mass of men who have followed the promoters, sustained them with their faith, with their loyalty and with their discipline, or criticised them "realistically" by dispersing or by remaining passive in response to some lead. But will this mass only consist of the party members? Will it be enough to follow the congresses, votes, etc., i.e. the whole of the activity and modes of existence through which a party mass shows its will? Obviously it will be necessary to take account of the social group of which the given party is the expression and the most advanced part: the history of a party, in other words, must be the history of a particular social group. But this group is not isolated; it has friends, allies, opponents and enemies. Only from the complex picture of social and State life (often even with international ramifications) will emerge the history of a certain party. It can therefore be said that to write the history of a party means in fact to write the general history of a country from a monographic point of view, in order to bring out a characteristic aspect. A party will have greater or less significance and weight, precisely to the extent to which its particular activity has weighed more or less in determining the history of a country.

That is why one's conception of what a party is and ought to be results from the way in which one writes the history of a party. The sectarian will rejoice in minor internal facts, which will have for him an esoteric significance and will fill him with mystical enthusiasm; the historian, however, who gives to everything the importance which it has in the general picture, will concentrate above all on the real efficacy of the party, on its determining power, positive or negative, in having contributed to creating an event or in having prevented other events from coming about.

The point of knowing when a party was formed, i.e. acquired a precise and permanent task, gives rise to many discussions and often also, only too often, to a form of arrogance, which is no less ridiculous and dangerous than the "national arrogance" of which Vico speaks. True, it can be said that a party is never completely formed, in the sense that every development creates new tasks and functions, and in the sense that for certain parties the paradox is true that they are completed and formed only when they no longer exist, i.e. when their existence has become historically useless. Thus, since every party is only a class nomenclature, it is evident that for the party which sets itself to abolish the division into classes, its perfection and completion consists in no longer existing, since classes, and therefore their expressions, no longer exist. But here I want to emphasise a particular stage in this process of development, the stage following that in which a fact may or may not exist, in the sense that the necessity for its existence has not yet become "peremptory", but depends in "great part" on the existence of persons of extraordinary will-power.

When does a party become historically "necessary"? When the conditions for its "triumphs", for its inevitable assumption of State Power are at least in process of formation and allow their further developments to be normally forseen. But then can one say, in these conditions, that a party cannot be destroyed by normal means? To answer this it is necessary to develop the argument: in order that a party shall exist the converging of three fundamental elements (i.e. of three groups of elements) is necessary:

(1) A widespread element of common, average men, whose participation is provided by discipline and faith, not by a creative and highly organisational spirit. Without these the party would not exist, it is true, but it is also true that the party would not exist "only" with these. They are a force in so far as there is someone who centralises, organises, disciplines them, and in the absence of this force they would break up and cancel each other out in scattered impotence. I do not deny that every one of these elements could become a cohesive force, but we are speaking of them precisely at the stage when they are not this and are not in a condition to be so, or if they are it is only in a restricted circle, politically ineffective, and inconsequential.

(2) The principal cohesive element, which centralises in the national field, which renders effective and powerful the totality of forces which left to themselves would count for nothing or very little; this element is endowed with a highly cohesive, centralising and disciplinary power which is also, perhaps because of this, inventive (if what is meant is "inventive" in a certain direction according to certain lines of force, certain perspectives and certain premises). It is also true that this element alone would not form a party, but it would do so more than the first element. They would be generals without an army, but in reality it is easier to create an army than to create generals. It is equally true that an already existing army is destroyed if the generals disappear, while the existence of a group of generals, trained to work together, in agreement among themselves, with common ends, is not slow to form an army even where none exists.

(3) A middle element, which links the first element with the second, and puts them into contact, not only "physically" but morally and intellectually. In fact, for every party there exist "definite proportions" between these three elements and the greatest effectiveness is achieved when these "definite proportions" are realised. Given these conditions one can say that a party cannot be destroyed by normal means, since

if there necessarily exists the second element, whose origin is tied to the existence of the objective material conditions, although in a dispersed and vague state (and if this second element does not exist all argument is pointless), then the other two elements cannot help being formed, i.e. the first element which necessarily forms the third as its continuation and means of expression.

For this to come about it is necessary that the iron conviction be formed that a certain solution to vital problems is necessary. Without this conviction the second element, whose destruction is easier on account of its smaller numbers, will not be formed, but it is necessary that this second element, if destroyed, leaves as an inheritance a ferment from which it can be reformed. And where can this ferment exist better and be able to form itself better than in the first and third elements, which, evidently, are the most homogeneous with the second? The activity of the second element to constitute this is therefore fundamental: the criterion of judgment of this second element is to be looked for: (1) in what it actually does; (2) in what it prepares on the hypothesis of its own destruction. Of the two facts it is difficult to say which is the more important. Since defeat in the struggle must always be forseen, the preparation of its own successors must be an element of equal importance with what is done for victory.

As regards party "arrogance", this may be said to be worse than the "national arrogance" of which Vico speaks. Why? Because a nation cannot help existing and in the fact that it exists it is always possible, even with good will and bringing forward authorities, to find that this existence is full of destiny and significance. On the other hand a party can cease to exist by its own act. It must *never* be forgotten that, in the struggle between nations, it is in the interest of each nation that the other should be weakened by internal struggles and that the parties are precisely the elements of internal struggles. For the parties, therefore, it is always possible to ask whether they exist by their own powers, as real necessity, or whether they exist only for the interests of others (and in fact in polemics this point is never forgotten, rather is it a persistent theme, especially when the reply is not in doubt, which means that it has been in doubt but is so no longer). Naturally the person who lets himself be torn to pieces by these doubts would be a fool. Politically the question has only a momentary relevance. In the history of the so-called principle of nationality, foreign interventions in favour of national parties which disturbed the internal order of antagonistic States are innumerable, so much so that when we speak, for example, of Cavour's "Eastern" policy we wonder whether we are speaking of a permanent line of action, or of a strategem of the moment to weaken Austria in view of 1859 and 1866. Thus in the Mazzinian movement of the early 1870's (for example, the Barsanti affair), we see the intervention of Bismarck, who in view of the war with France and the danger of a Franco-Italian alliance, thought to weaken Italy by internal conflicts. Thus, in the events of June, 1914 some see the intervention of the Austrian General Staff in the light of the war to come. As we see, the casuistry takes many forms, and it is necessary to have clear ideas about it. Admitted that whatever one does, one always plays somebody's game, the important thing is to seek in every way to play one's own game, i.e. to win completely. Anyway, we must despise party "arrogance" and substitute for it concrete facts. Those who substitute arrogance for facts, or carry on a policy of arrogance, are certainly to be suspected of very little seriousness. It is not necessary to add that it is essential for parties to avoid even the "justified" appearance of playing somebody else's game, especially if the somebody is a foreign State; but if someone tries to exploit this nothing can be done about it.

It is difficult to exclude the fact that some political parties (of the ruling group but also of subordinate groups) also fulfil a police function, that is, one of tutelage to a certain political and legal order. If this were shown, with precision, the question would have to be posed in other terms: i.e. about the ways and directions in which this function comes to be exercised. Is the sense repressive or propagandist, i.e. is it of a reactionary or a progressive character? Does the given party exercise its police function by conserving an external, extrinsic order, as tethering rope of the live forces of history, or does it do so by aiming to raise the people to a new level of civilisation whose political and legal order is a programmatic expression? In fact, a law finds out the people who break it: (1) among the socially reactionary elements whom the law has dispossessed; (2) among the progressive elements whom the law represses; (3) among the elements who have not reached the level of civilisation which the law may represent. The police function of a party can therefore be progressive or regressive: it is progressive when it aims to keep the reactionary forces inside the orbit of legality and to raise the backward masses to the level of the new legality. It is regressive when it aims to repress the live forces of society and maintain a superseded, anti-historic legality which has become extrinsic. For the rest, the functioning of a given party furnishes discriminating criteria: when a party is progressive it functions "democratically" (in accordance with democratic centralism), when it is regressive it functions "bureaucratically" (in the sense of bureaucratic centralism). The party in this second case is purely executive, not deliberative: it is then technically a police organisation and its name of "political party" is pure mythological metaphor.

## Some Theoretical and Practical Aspects of "Economism"

Economism—theoretical movement for free trade—theoretical syndicalism. It is to be seen to what extent theoretical syndicalism originated from Marxism and how far from the economic doctrines of free trade, i.e. in the last analysis, from liberalism. And therefore it is to be seen whether economism, in its most complete form, is not a direct offspring of liberalism, and had, even in its origins, very little relationship with Marxism, a relation at any rate of an extrinsic and purely verbal kind.

The standpoint of the movement for free trade is based on a theoretical error whose practical origin it is not difficult to identify: on the distinction, that is, between political society and civil society, which from being a methodological distinction becomes, and is presented as, an organic distinction. Thus it is asserted that economic activity concerns civil society and that the State must not intervene in its regulation. But, as in actual reality civil society and the State are identified, it must be settled that even liberalism is a form of "regulation" of a State kind, introduced and maintained by means of legislation and coercion: it is an act of will conscious of its own ends and not the spontaneous, automatic expression of an economic fact. Therefore liberalism is a political programme, destined to change, in so far as it triumphs, the leading personnel of the State and the economic programme of the State itself, in other words, to alter the distribution of the national income.

The case of theoretical syndicalism is different, in that it relates to a subordinate group, which is prevented by this theory from ever becoming dominant, of developing beyond the economico-corporative phase in order to raise itself to the phase of ethico-political hegemony in civil society and of domination in the State. As far as liberalism is concerned it is a case of a fraction of the ruling group which wants to modify, not the structure of the State, but only the direction of government, which wants to reform commercial legislation and only indirectly industrial legislation (since it is undeniable that protection, especially in countries with a poor and restricted market, limits freedom of industrial initiative and unhealthily favours the origin of monopolies): it is a question of a rotation of the leading parties in the government, not of the foundation and organisation of a new political society and even less of a new type of civil society. In the theoretical syndicalist movement the question arises in a more complex form; it is undeniable that in it the independence and autonomy of the subordinate group, which it professes to express, are in fact sacrificed to the intellectual hegemony of the ruling group, precisely because syndicalism is only an aspect of liberalism, justified by a few mutilated and therefore banal quotations from Marxism. Why and how does this "sacrifice" come about? The transformation of the subordinate into the ruling group is excluded, either because the problem is not even seen (Fabianism, De Man, an important part of the Labour Party), or because it is presented in inconsistent and ineffective ways (social-democratic tendencies in general), or because an immediate leap from a class régime to one of perfect equality and syndical economy is postulated.

The standpoint of economism towards expressions of will, of action and of political and intellectual initiative, as if these were a necessary emanation of economics and, moreover, the sole effective expression of the economy, is, to say the least, strange; thus it is inconsistent that the concrete posing of the question of hegemony should be interpreted as a fact which subordinates the hegemonous group. The fact of hegemony undoubtedly presupposes that the interests and strivings of the groups over which the hegemony will be exercised are taken account of, that a certain balance of compromises be formed, that, in other words, the leading group makes some sacrifices of an economico-corporative kind; but it is also undoubted that these sacrifices and compromises cannot concern essentials, since if the hegemony is ethico-political, it must also be economic, it must have its foundation in the decisive function that the leading group exercises in the decisive sphere of economic activity.

Economism presents itself in many other different forms besides liberalism and theoretical syndicalism. All forms of electoral abstention belong to it (a typical example is the abstention of the Italian Clericals after 1870, which steadily diminished after 1900 until 1919 and the formation of the Popular Party: the distinction which the Clericals made between real Italy and legal Italy was a reproduction of the distinction between the economic and the politico-legal world); and there are many forms of electoral abstention, since there can also be semi-abstention, quarter, etc. Abstention is linked with the formula "so much the worse, so much the better", and also the formula of the so-called parliamentary "intransigence" of some groups of deputies. Economism is not always against political action and the political party, but the latter is considered as merely an educational organisation of a syndical type. One point of reference for the study of economism and for understanding the relationship between structure and superstructure is that passage from *The Poverty of Philosophy*, where Marx says that an important phase in the development of the social group is that in which the single components of a trade union do not struggle any longer only for their own economic interests, but for the defence and development of the organisation itself.[1] This should be remembered together with Engels' statement that only in the "last analysis" is the economy the mainspring of history (in his two letters on Marxism published also in Italian),[2] and taken together with the passage in the

[1] See the exact statement (*Poverty of Philosophy*, English edition, Moscow, 1956, pp. 194-5.) *The Poverty of Philosophy* is an essential stage of the formation of Marxism; it can be considered as a development of the *Theses on Feuerbach*, whereas the *Holy Family* is an indistinct, intermediate phase of haphazard origin, as appears from the parts dedicated to Proudhon and especially to French materialism. The section on French materialism is more than anything else a chapter in the history of culture and is not theoretical, as it has often been interpreted, and as history of culture it is admirable. Remember the observation that the criticism of Proudhon and his interpretation of the Hegelian dialectic in *The Poverty of Philosophy* can be extended to Gioberti and to the Hegelianism of the moderate Italian Liberals in general. The parallel Proudhon-Gioberti, although they represent historico-political phases which are not homogeneous, or rather precisely because of this, may be interesting and fertile.

[2] *Marx-Engels Selected Works*, English edition, p. 443 and p. 445.

Preface to the *Critique of Political Economy* where it says that it is in the field of ideologies that men become aware of the conflict which takes place in the economic world.

On various occasions it has been stated in these notes that Marxism is much more widespread than is generally conceded. The assertion is correct if what is meant is that historical economism is widespread, as Professor Loria now calls his more or less clumsy conceptions, and that therefore the cultural environment has completely changed from the time when Marxism began its struggles; it could be said, in Crocian terminology, that the greatest heresy arisen from the womb of "the religion of liberty" has also like orthodox religion, suffered degeneration, has been propagated as "superstition", i.e. it has entered into a combination with liberalism and produced economism. But it should be seen whether, while the orthodox religion has shrivelled up, the heretical superstition has not always maintained a ferment which will give it a new birth as a higher religion; whether, that is, the slag of superstition can easily be liquidated.

Some characteristic points of historical economism: (1) in research for historical connections it does not distinguish what is "relatively permanent" from what is an occasional fluctuation, and by an economic fact it means the personal self-interest of a small group, in a direct and "dirty Jewish" sense. In other words, it does not take account of the formations of economic classes, with all their inherent relationships, but assumes a mean and usurious self-interest, especially when this takes on criminal forms; (2) the doctrine by which economic development is reduced to a succession of technical changes in the instruments of labour. The discovery of new combustibles and of new motive energies, as of new raw materials to be transformed, has a certain great importance, since it can alter the position of individual States, but it does not determine the historical movement, etc.

It often happens that people attack historical economism believing that they are attacking historical materialism. This is the case, for example, in an article in *Avenir* of Paris for October 10th, 1930 (reported in *The Weekly Review of the Foreign Press* for October 21st, 1930, pp. 2303-4) which I quote as typical: "We have been told for a long time, but especially since the war, that questions of self-interest dominate the peoples and lead the world forward. It is the Marxists who have invented this thesis, under the slightly doctrinaire name of 'historical materialism'. In pure Marxism, men taken in the mass do not obey passions but economic necessity. Politics is passion. Patriotism is passion. These two necessary ideas only enjoy an apparent function in history because in reality the life of the peoples, throughout the centuries, is explained by a changing and ever renewed interplay of causes of an economic kind. Economics is everything. Many philosophers and 'bourgeois' economists have taken up this refrain. They assume a certain air of explaining international politics to us by competition for grain, petrol or rubber. They exert themselves to explain to us that all diplomacy is governed by questions of customs duties and cost prices. These explanations are very much in the ascendant. They have a slightly scientific appearance and proceed from a kind of superior scepticism which would like to pass for supreme smartness. Passion in foreign policy? Sentiment in home affairs? Away with it! That stuff is all right for simpletons. The great minds, the initiated, know that everything is governed by supply and demand. Now this is an absolute pseudo-truth. It is utterly false that the peoples only let themselves be led by considerations of self-interest and it is entirely true that they obey above all considerations dictated by a desire for and an ardent faith in prestige. Anyone who does not understand this understands nothing." The rest of the article (entitled "The mania for prestige") gives the example of German and Italian policy which, it says, is dictated by "prestige" and not by material interests. The article contains in brief a large dose of the more banal polemical points against Marxism, but in reality the polemic is against clumsy economism of the Loria type. On the other hand, the writer is not very strong in argument even in other respects: he does not understand that "passion" could be simply a synonym for economic interest and that it is difficult to maintain that political activity is a permanent state of passionate exasperation and agony; French politics is actually represented as systematic and coherent "rationality", purged of all passionate elements, etc.

In its most widespread form of economist superstition, Marxism loses a great part of its cultural expansiveness in the higher sphere of the intellectual group, in return for what it gains among the popular masses and the mediocre intellectuals, who like to appear very cunning but who do not intend to overtax their brains, etc. As Engels wrote, it is very convenient for many people to believe that they have in their pockets, cheap and with no effort, the whole of history, all political and philosophical wisdom concentrated in a few formulæ. Forgetting that the thesis that men became conscious of the basic conflicts in the field of ideology, is not of a psychological or moralistic, but of an organic epistemological character, they create a *forma mentis* for considering politics and hence history as a continuous *marche des dupes*, a game of illusions and conjuring. "Critical" activity is reduced to exposing tricks, discovering scandals, prying into the pockets of representative men.

Thus it is forgotten that since "economism" is, or is presumed to be, also an objective canon of interpretation (objective-scientific), the search for immediate self-interest must be valid for all aspects of history, for the men who represent the "thesis" as well as for those who represent the "antithesis". In addition another proposition of Marxism is also forgotten: the proposition that "popular beliefs" or beliefs of the same kind as popular beliefs have the validity of material forces. The errors of interpretation in this research for "dirty Jewish" self-interests have sometimes been crude and comical and so have reacted negatively on the prestige of the original doctrine. It is therefore necessary to fight against economism not only in the theory of historiography, but also and especially in the theory and practice of politics. In this field, the struggle can and must be conducted by developing the theory of the political party and by the practical development of the life of certain political parties (the struggle against the theory of the so-called permanent revolution, to which is opposed the concept of revolutionary democratic dictatorship, the importance received by the support given to constituent ideologies, etc.). One could research into the judgments that emerged as to how certain political movements developed, taking as typical the Boulangist movement (from 1886 to about 1890) or the Dreyfus affair or even the *coup d'état* of December 2nd (an analysis of Marx's classic book *The Eighteenth Brumaire of Louis Bonaparte*), to study what relative importance is given to the immediate economic factor and what space is occupied by the concrete study of "ideologies". Faced with these events, economism asks the question: who enjoyed the immediate initiative in the matter? And answers it with arguments as naïve as they are paralogistic. It was enjoyed immediately by a certain fraction of the ruling group and in order not to make a mistake this choice falls on that fraction which evidently has a progressive function and one of control over all the economic forces. One can be sure of not being wrong, because necessarily, if the movement under examination comes to power, sooner or later the progressive faction of the ruling group will end up by controlling the new government and by making it its instrument for wielding the state apparatus to its own benefit.

This, therefore, is a very cheap infallibility which not only has no theoretical significance, but has very little political importance and practical efficacy: in general it does not produce anything except moralistic sermons and interminable personal problems. When a movement of the Boulangist type is produced, the analysis should be realistically conducted along these lines: (1) The social content of the masses who adhere to the movement; (2) What function these masses have in the balance of forces, which is being transformed, as is shown by the very birth of the new movement? (3) What political and social significance have the aims which the leaders present and which find consent? To what effective needs do they correspond? (4) Examination of the means for the proposed end; (5) Only in the last analysis, and in a political and not a moralistic form, does one put forward the *hypothesis* that this movement will necessarily be changed in nature, and serve very different ends from those which the following multitudes expect. But with the economists, this hypothesis is asserted in anticipation, when no concrete element (one which, in other words, appears as such on the evidence of common sense and not from some esoterically "scientific" analysis) yet exists to support it, so that it appears as a moralistic accusation of duplicity and bad faith or of lack of shrewdness or of stupidity (on the part of the followers). The political struggle thus becomes a series of personal encounters between those who are not taken in, and who "have the devil in the bottle", and those who are made fools of by their own leaders and are unwilling to be convinced because of their incurable foolishness. On the other hand, until these movements have achieved power it can always be thought that they may fail, and some indeed have failed (Boulangism itself, which failed as such and was later definitely crushed by the Dreyfusard movement; the movement of George Valois; that of General Gayda); research must therefore be directed to the identification of the elements of power, but also of the elements of weakness which they contain within them: the "economist" hypothesis asserts an immediate element of power, i.e. the availability of certain direct or indirect financial support (a large newspaper which backs up the movement is also a financial support) and that is all. It is too little. In this case also the analysis of the different levels of relations of forces can only culminate in the sphere of hegemony and of ethico-political relationships.

An element to be added as exemplifying theories of so-called intransigence is that of rigid aversion on principle to so-called compromises, which has as a subordinate manifestation what can be called the "fear of dangers". It is clear that the aversion on principle to compromises is closely tied to economism, in that the conception on which this aversion is based cannot be other than the iron conviction that there exist objective laws for historical development of the same character as natural laws, with, in addition, the belief in a fatalistic finalism of a similar character to religious belief: since the favourable conditions are predestined to come into existence and from these will be determined, in a somewhat mysterious way, regenerative events. The result is not only uselessness but the loss of all voluntary initiative aiming to predispose this situation according to a plan. Side by side with these fatalistic convictions is nevertheless the tendency to trust "for the future" blindly and uncritically in the regulating virtue of arms, though this is not completely without logic and coherence, since the intervention of the will is thought to be useful for destruction, not for construction (already in action at the very moment of destruction). Destruction is conceived mechanically, not as destruction-construction. In such ways of thinking no account is taken of the "time" factor and no account is taken, in the last analysis, of the "economy" itself, in the sense that there is no understanding of how mass ideological facts always lag behind mass economic phenomena and how, therefore, at certain moments the automatic drive due to the economic factor is slowed down, cramped or even broken up momentarily by traditional ideological elements. There must, therefore, be a consciously planned struggle to win "understanding" of the requirements of the economic position of the masses which may be opposed to the directives of the traditional leaders. An appropriate political initiative is always necessary to free the economic drive from the tethers of traditional policies, to change, that is, the political direction of certain forces which must be absorbed in order to realise a new, homogeneous, economico-political historical *bloc*, without internal contradictions; and since two "similar" forces can only be fused in the new organism through a series of compromises or by force of arms, coming together on a plan of alliance or by subordinating one to the other with coercion, the question is whether one has this force and whether it is "productive" to employ it. If the union of two forces is necessary in order to conquer a third, the recourse to arms and coercion (given that these are available) is a purely methodological hypothesis and the only concrete possibility is compromise, since force can be employed against enemies, not against a part of oneself which one wants to assimilate rapidly, for which "good will" and enthusiasm are necessary.

### Foresight and Perspective

Another point to be decided and developed is that of the "double perspective" in political action and state life. There are various levels in which the double perspective can be presented, from the most elementary to the most complex, but they can be reduced theoretically to two fundamental levels, corresponding to the double nature of the Machiavellian Centaur, savage and human, force and consent, authority and hegemony, violence and civilisation, the individual stage and the universal stage ("Church" and "State"), agitation and propaganda, tactics and strategy, etc. Some people have reduced the theory of the "double perspective" to something paltry and banal, that is, to nothing but two forms of "immediacy" which follow each other mechanically in time with greater or less "proximity". But it can happen that the more the first "perspective" is "very immediate", very elementary, the more "distant" must be the second (not in time, but as a dialectical relationship), the more complex, elevated; in other words it may happen, as in human life, that the more an individual is constrained to defend his own immediate physical existence, the more he sustains and sees himself from the point of view of all the complex and most elevated values of civilisation and humanity.

It is certain that to foresee means only to see well the present and the past as movement: to see well, i.e. to identify with exactness the fundamental and permanent elements of the process. But it is absurd to think of a purely "objective" foresight. The person who has foresight in reality has a "programme" that he wants to see triumph, and foresight is precisely an element of this triumph. This only means that foresight must always be either arbitrary and gratuitous or purely tendentious. Moreover, once can say that only to the extent to which the objective aspect of foresight is connected with a programme, does this aspect acquire objectivity: (1) because only passion sharpens the intellect and co-operates in making intuition clearer; (2) because since reality is the result of the application of human will to the society of things (of the worker to the machine), to put aside every voluntary element and calculate only the intervention of other wills as an objective element in the general game is to mutilate reality itself. Only those who strongly want to do it identify the necessary elements for the realisation of their will.

Therefore, to hold that one particular conception of the world and of life has in itself a superior capacity for foresight is a mistake of the crudest fatuity and superficiality. Certainly a conception of the world is implicit in all foresight and therefore whether this is a disconnected series of arbitrary acts of thought or a rigorous and coherent vision is not without importance, but it acquires importance precisely in the living brain of the person who makes the prophesy and brings it to life with his own strong will. We see this from the prophesies made by so-called "dispassionate" people: they abound in indolence, minute subtleties, conjectural elegances. The existence of a programme to be realised by the "foreseer" is enough for him to reach the essentials, those elements which, being "organisable", susceptible to be directed or redirected, are in reality alone foreseeable. This conflicts with the common way of considering the problem. It is generally thought that every act of foresight presupposes the determination of regular laws of the same type as the laws of the natural sciences. But just as these laws do not exist in the absolute or mechanical sense which is supposed, so also this view takes no account of the other wills and their application is not "foreseen". Because of this, constructions are made on an arbitrary hypothesis and not on reality.

"Too much" (and therefore superficial and mechanical) political realism, often leads to the assertion that the man of State must work only within the sphere of "effective reality", not interest himself in "what should be", but only in "what is". This would mean that the man of State must have no perspectives longer than his own nose. This error has led Paolo Treves to see in Guicciardini and not in Machiavelli the "true politician".

It is necessary to distinguish between the scientist of politics and the active politician, as well as between the "diplomat" and the "politician". The diplomat can only move within effective reality, since his specific activity is not that of looking for new equilibriums, but of conserving an existing equilibrium within a certain judicial framework. Thus also the scientist must only move inside effective reality in so far as he is merely a scientist. But Machiavelli is not merely a scientist; he is a partisan, with mighty passions, an active politician, who wants to create new relations of forces and because of this cannot help concerning himself with "what should be", though certainly not in the moralistic sense. The question is not therefore to be put in these terms, it is more complex: the point is, in other words, to see whether "what should be" is an arbitrary or necessary act, concrete will or a hopeless wish, a desire, a yearning for the stars. The active politician is a creator, an awakener, but he neither creates from nothing nor moves in the turbid void of his own desires and dreams. He bases himself on effective reality, but what is this effective reality? Is it something static and immobile or is it not rather a relationship of forces in continuous movement and change of equilibrium? To apply the will to the creation of a new balance of the really existing and operating forces, basing oneself on that particular force which one considers progressive, giving it the means to triumph, is still to move within the sphere of effective reality, but in order to dominate and overcome it (or contribute to this). "What should be" is therefore concrete, and is moreover the only realistic and historicist interpretation of reality; it is the only active history and philosophy, the only politics.

The Savonarola-Machiavelli opposition is not an opposition between what is and what should be (the whole of Russo's paragraph on this point is simply word-show) but between two should-be's, the abstract and cloudy one of Savonarola and the realistic one of Machiavelli, realistic even if it did not become immediate reality, since one cannot expect one individual or one book to change reality but only to interpret it and indicate the possible lines of action. Machiavelli's limits and narrowness consist only in his having been a "private person", a writer, and not the head of a State or an army, who is still a single person but who has at his disposal the forces of the State or an army and not only armies of words. One cannot therefore say that Machiavelli was also an "unarmed prophet": this would be to belittle the spirit. Machiavelli never says that he is thinking of changing, or that he has set himself to change, reality, but only that he is showing concretely how the historical forces ought to have worked in order to be effective.

### Analysis of Situations. Relations of Forces

The study of how "situations" need to be analysed, i.e. of how the different levels of the relations of forces need to be established, can lend itself to an elementary exposition of the science and art of politics, in the sense of the totality of practical canons for research and of particular observations useful for awakening interest in effective reality and encouraging more rigorous and vigorous political intuitions. At the same time an exposition should be made of what must be understood by strategy and tactics, by strategic "plan", by propaganda and agitation, by the science of organisation and administration in politics. The empirical observations which are usually expounded here and there in works on political science (as for example in G. Mosca's book, *The Elements of Political Science*) ought, in so far as they are not abstract matters or with no solid foundation, to find a place in the different levels of the relations of forces, beginning with the relations of international forces and going on to the objective social relations, i.e. to the level of development of the productive forces, to the relations of political and party forces (hegemonic systems inside the State) and to the immediate (or potentially military) political relations.

Do international relations precede or follow (logically) the fundamental social relations? Undoubtedly they follow. Every organic innovation in the structure modifies organically the *absolute* and *relative* relations in the international field, through its technico-military expressions. Even the geographical position of a national State does not precede but follows (logically) the structural innovations, though reacting on them to a certain extent (to the extent precisely to which superstructures react on the structure, politics on economics, etc.). On the other hand international relations react passively and actively on the political relations (of hegemony of parties). The more the immediate economic life of a nation is subordinated to international relations, the more a certain party will represent this situation and exploit it in order to prevent any advantage for the opposing parties (remember Nitti's famous speech about the *technically* impossible Italian revolution!). From this series of facts the conclusion can be reached that often the so-called "foreigners' party" is not the same as it is popularly called, but is in fact the most nationalistic party, which, in reality, rather than representing the vital forces of its own country, represents its subordination and economic slavery to the hegemonic nations or groups of nations.

It is the problem of the relations between structure and superstructures which needs to be posed exactly and resolved in order to reach a correct analysis of the forces working in the history of a certain period and determine their relationship. One must keep within the bounds of two principles: (1) that no society sets itself tasks for whose solution the necessary and sufficient conditions do not already exist or are not at least in process of emergence and development; (2) that no society dissolves and can be replaced unless it has first developed all the forms of life implicit in its relations.[1] From reflection on these two canons one can successfully develop a whole series of other principles of historical methodology. However, in studying a structure, it is necessary to distinguish organic movements (relatively permanent) from movements which could be called "incidental" (which appear as occasional, immediate, almost accidental). Incidental phenomena are certainly dependent as well on the organic movements, but their significance has no great historical importance: they give rise to a petty, day-to-day political criticism which concerns the small ruling

[1] "No social order ever perishes before all the productive forces for which there is room in it have developed; and new, higher relations of production never appear before the material conditions for their existence have matured in the womb of the old society. Therefore mankind always sets itself only such tasks as it can solve; since, looking at the matter more closely, it will always be found that the task itself arises only when the material conditions for its solution already exist or are at least in the process of formation." Marx, Preface to *The Critique of Political Economy*.

groups and personalities directly responsible for power. Organic phenomena give rise to historico-social criticism which concerns the large groupings, those beyond the immediately responsible people and beyond the leading personnel. In studying an historical period this distinction appears of the greatest importance. A crisis appears which sometimes lasts for decades. This exceptional duration means that incurable contradictions have appeared (have come to maturity) in the structure, and that the political forces working positively for the preservation and defence of the same structure are exerting themselves nevertheless to heal them within certain limits and to overcome them. These incessant and persistent efforts (since no social form is ever willing to confess that is has been superseded), form the basis for the "occasional" ("*occasionale*"), on which was organised the antagonistic forces which aim to show (a demonstration which in the last analysis only succeeds and is "true" if it becomes a new reality, if the antagonistic forces triumph, whereas in the short term there develops a whole series of ideological, religious, philosophical, political, legal, etc., polemics whose concreteness is to be valued by the extent to which they succeed in conquering and in displacing the existing array of social forces) that the necessary and sufficient conditions already exist which make possible and imperative the historical solution of certain tasks (imperative, because every shortcoming in historical duty increases the necessary disorder and prepares more serious catastrophes).

The error often committed in historico-political analyses consists in having been unable to find the correct relationship between what is organic and what is occasional: thus one succeeds either in expounding as directly operative causes which instead operate indirectly, or in asserting that direct causes are the only effective causes; in one case there is an excess of "economism" or pedantic doctrinairism, in the other an excess of "ideologism"; in the one case an overestimation of mechanical causes, in the other an exaltation of the voluntarist and individual element. The distinction between organic "movements" and events and "incidental" or occasional movements and events must be applied to all type of situations, not only to those where one sees a reactionary development or an acute crisis, but to those where one sees a progressive or prosperous development and to those where one sees a stagnation of the productive forces. The dialectical nexus

between the two kinds of movement, and, therefore, of research, is
difficult to establish; and, if the error is serious in historiography, it is
still more serious in the art of politics, where we are dealing not with
reconstructing past history but with building present and future
history:[1] one's own inferior and immediate desires and passions are
the cause of error, in so far as they are substituted for objective and
impartial analysis, and this happens not as a conscious "means" to
stimulate action but as self-deceit. Here also, the snake bites the char-
latan, or rather the demagogue is the first victim of his demagogy.

These methodological criteria acquire their full significance only if
applied to the examination of concrete historical events. This could be
usefully done for the events unfolded in France from 1789 to 1870. I
think that, for greater clarity in the exposition, it is really necessary to
take in the whole of this period. Indeed, only in 1870-1, with the
Communard attempt, were all the germs born in 1789 historically
worked out, in other words, not only did the new class struggling for
power conquer the representatives of the old society who did not wish
to admit that they had been decisively overcome, but it also conquered
the newest groups which held that the new structure which had arisen
out of the development begun in 1789 was already outdated, and thus
showed that it was alive in comparison with both the old and the very
new. Further, with 1870-1 all the principles of political strategy and
tactics born in practice in 1789 and developed ideologically around
1848 lost their efficacy (those which are summed up in the formula of
the "permanent revolution";[2] it would be interesting to study how far
this formula passed into Mazzini's strategy—for example, the Milan

[1] Failure to consider the immediate stage of the "relation of forces" is linked with
hangovers of the popular liberal conception, of which syndicalism is a manifestation,
believing that it is more advanced while in reality it took a step backwards. In fact the
popular liberal conception giving importance to the relation of political forces organised
in the various forms of party (newspaper-readers, parliamentary and local elections, mass
organisations of parties and trade unions in the narrow sense) was more advanced than
syndicalism, which gave primordial importance to the fundamental economico-social
relations and only to these. The popular liberal conception implicitly took account of
these relations also (as appears from many signs), but insisted more on the relations of
political forces which were the expression of the former and in reality contained them.
These hangovers of the popular liberal conception can be traced back to a whole series of
writings which purport to be connected with Marxism and have given rise to infantile
forms of optimism and folly.

[2] The term "permanent revolution" is used here by Gramsci to indicate the interpretation given by Trotsky (i.e. of a political revolution achieved by a minority without
the support of the great masses) to this formula of Karl Marx. It is for this reason that
Gramsci puts it in inverted commas.—*Trans.*

insurrection of 1853—and whether this took place consciously or otherwise). An element showing the correctness of this point of view is the fact that historians are in no way in agreement (and it is impossible that they should be) in fixing the limits for that group of events which constitutes the French Revolution. For some (e.g. Salvemini), the Revolution was completed at Valmy: France had created a new State and had been able to organise the politico-military force to assert and defend its territorial sovereignty. For others the Revolution continued until Thermidor, and, moreover, they speak of more revolutions (August 10th is, according to them, a revolution in itself, etc.).[1] The method of interpreting Thermidor and the work of Napoleon provides the sharpest contradictions: is it revolution or counter-revolution? For others the history of the Revolution continues down to 1830, 1848, 1870 and even until the Great War of 1914. In all these views there is some truth. Really the internal contradictions of French social structure which develop after 1789 are relatively composed only in the Third Republic and France has sixty years of balanced political life after eighty of ever longer waves of revolution: 1789, '94, '99, 1804, '15, '30, '48, '70. It is precisely the study of these "waves" of varying frequency which allows us to reconstruct the relations between structure and superstructure, on the one hand, and, on the other, between the development of organic movement and incidental movement in the structure. It can at the same time be said that the dialectical interaction between the two methodological principles put forward at the beginning of this note can be found in the politico-historical formula of permanent revolution.

An aspect of the same problem is the so-called question of the relations of forces. One often reads in historical narratives expressions like: "favourable relations of forces, unfavourable to this or that tendency". Thus, abstractly, this formulation explains nothing or almost nothing, since all it does is to repeat the fact which ought to be explained, presenting it once as a fact and once as an abstract law, as an explanation. The theoretical error consists therefore in giving a canon of research and interpretation as an "historical cause".

At the same time it is necessary to distinguish different stages and levels in the "relation of forces", which fundamentally are the following:

[1] cf. *The French Revolution*, by A. Mathiez.

(1) A relation of social forces closely tied to the structure, objective, independent of men's will, which can be measured with the precision of the exact or physical sciences. On the basis of the level of development of the material forces of production we have social classes, each one of which represents a function and has a given position in production itself. This relation is what it is, stubborn reality: no one can change the number of factories and their workers, the number of cities with a given urban population, etc. This fundamental scheme enables us to study whether there exist in the society the necessary and sufficient conditions for its transformation, enables us, that is, to check the level of reality and attainability of the different ideologies which have come into existence on the same basis, on the basis of the contradictions which it has generated in the course of its development.

(2) A later stage is the relation of political forces; that is to say, an estimation of the degree of homogeneity, of self-consciousness and organisation reached by the various social groups. This stage can be in its turn analysed and differentiated into various levels, corresponding to the different degrees of collective self-consciousness, as they have manifested themselves up to now in history. The first and most elementary is the economico-corporative stage: one trader feels that he *must* be solid with another trader, one manufacturer with another; in other words a homogeneous unity is felt, and the duty to organise it, by the professional group, but not yet by the wider social group. A second stage is that in which consciousness of the solidarity of interests among all the members of the social group is reached, but still in the purely economic field. Already at this stage the question of the State is posed, but only on the basis of reaching a politico-legal equality with the ruling group, since the right is proclaimed to share in legislation and administration and even to modify it, reform it, but inside the fundamental existing framework. A third stage is that in which consciousness is reached that one's own corporative interests, in their present and future development, transcend the corporative circle of the purely economic group, and can and must become the interests of other subordinate groups. This is the more strictly political phase, which marks the clear transition from the structure to the sphere of complex superstructures, it is the phase in which ideologies which were germinated earlier become "party", come into opposition and

enter the struggle until the point is reached where one of them or at least one combination of them, tends to predominate, to impose itself, to propogate itself throughout the whole social sphere, causing, in addition to singleness of economic and political purpose, an intellectual and moral unity as well, placing all questions around which the struggle rages not on a corporative, but a "universal" plane and creating in this way the hegemony of a fundamental social group over a number of subordinate groups. The State is conceived, certainly, as an organism belonging to a group, destined to create the conditions favourable to the greatest expansion of that group; but this development and expansion are conceived and presented as the motive force of a universal expansion, of a development of all the "national" energies; that is to to say, the ruling group is co-ordinated concretely with the general interests of the subordinate groups and State life is conceived as a continual formation and overcoming of unstable equilibriums (unstable within the ambit of the law), between the interests of the fundamental group and those of the subordinate groups, equilibriums in which the interests of the ruling group predominate but only up to a certain point, i.e. not as far as their mean economico-corporative interest would like.

In historical reality these stages are reciprocally mixed, horizontally and vertically so to speak—according to economic and social activities (horizontally) and according to territory (vertically), combining and splitting up differently: each one of these combinations may be represented by its own organised economic and political expression. It is also necessary to take account of the fact that international relations are interlaced with these internal relations of a nation-State, creating new, original and historically concrete combinations. An ideology, coming into existence in a more developed country, is diffused in less developed countries cutting across the local play of combinations.

This relationship between international and national forces is again complicated by the existence inside each State of several territorial sections with a different structure and a different relation of forces at all levels (thus *La Vandée* was allied with reactionary international forces and represented them inside the bosom of French territorial unity; similarly Lyons in the French Revolution represented a particular knot of relations, etc.).

(3) The third stage is that of the relations of military forces, time and again immediately decisive. (Historical development oscillates continuously between the first and the third stage, with the mediation of the second.) But this also is not something indistinct and immediately identifiable in a schematic form; two levels can be distinguished: the military level in the strict or technico-military sense, and the level which can be called politico-military. In the development of history these two levels are presented in a great variety of combinations. A typical example which can serve as demonstration-limit, is that of the relationship of military oppression of a State over a nation which is seeking to achieve its State independence. The relationship is not purely military, but politico-military; and, in fact, such a type of oppression would be inexplicable without a state of social disintegration among the oppressed people and the passivity of the majority; because of this, independence cannot be achieved with purely military forces, but with military and politico-military forces. If the oppressed nation, in fact, in order to begin the struggle for independence, had to wait for the hegemonic State to allow it to organise its own army in the strict and technical sense of the word, it would have to wait quite a while (it might happen that the aim of having its own army could be granted by the hegemonic nation, but this means that already a great part of the struggle has been fought and won on the politico-military plane). The oppressed nation will therefore oppose the hegemonic military force initially with a force which is only "politico-military", that is, with a form of political action which has the virtue of causing repercussions of a military character in the sense (1) that it is effective in breaking up from the inside the war efficiency of the hegemonic nation; (2) that it obliges the hegemonic military force to dissolve and disperse itself over a large territory, nullifying the greater part of its war efficiency. In the Italian *Risorgimento* the disastrous absence of politico-military leadership can be noted, especially in the Party of Action (through congenital incapacity), but also in the Piedmontese moderate party, both before and after 1848, certainly not through incapacity, but through "economico-political Malthusianism", or in other words because it was unwilling even to mention the possibility of agrarian reform and because it did not want the calling of a constituent national assembly, but only aimed at extending the Piedmontese

monarchy, without limitations or conditions of popular origin, to the whole of Italy, solely with the sanction of regional plebiscites.

Another question connected with the preceding ones is that of seeing whether fundamental historical crises are directly caused by economic crises. The answer is contained implicitly in the preceding paragraphs, where we dealt with questions which are only another way of looking at the present one; nevertheless it is always necessary, for didactic reasons, given the particular public, to examine every way of presenting the same question as if it were an independent and new problem. It can be excluded that, by themselves, economic crises directly produce fundamental events; they can only create a more favourable ground for the propagation of certain ways of thinking, of posing and solving questions which involve the whole future development of State life. For the rest, all assertions regarding periods of crisis or prosperity can give rise to onesided judgments. Mathiez, in his review of the history of the French Revolution, opposing the popular traditional history, which "found" *a priori* a crisis coinciding with the great breach in the social equilibrium, asserts that around 1789 the economic situation was, on the contrary, good in the short run, and that therefore one cannot say that the catastrophe of the absolute State was due to a crisis of impoverishment. It needs to be observed that the State was in the grip of a deadly financial crisis and the question arose of which of the three privileged social orders ought to bear the sacrifices and burdens in order to put the State and Royal finances in order. Further: if the bourgeoisie was in a flourishing economic position, the popular classes of the cities and countryside were certainly not in a good situation, especially those who were racked by endemic poverty. In any case, the breach in the equilibrium of forces did not come about through the immediate mechanical cause of the impoverishment of the social group which had an interest in breaking the equilibrium and in fact did break it; it came about within the framework of conflicts above the immediate economic world, connected with the "prestige" of classes (future economic interests), with an exasperation of the feeling of independence, autonomy and power. The particular question of economic malaise or health as a cause of new historical realities is a partial aspect of the question of the relations of forces in their various levels. Changes can be produced either because a situation of well-being is threatened by the selfish egotism of an opposed group, or because malaise has become intolerable and one cannot see in the old society any force which is capable of mitigating it and re-establishing normality by legal means. One can therefore say that all these elements are the concrete manifestations of the incidental fluctuations of the totality of social relations of force, on the basis of which occurs the transition of the latter, to political relations of force, culminating in the decisive military relationship.

If this process of development from one stage to the other is lacking, and it is essentially a process which has for its actors men and the will and capacity of men, the situation remains static. Contradictory conclusions can arise: the old society resists and is helped by a "breathing space", physically exterminating the opposing *élite* and terrorising the masses of reserves; or the reciprocal destruction of the conflicting forces takes place with the establishment of the peace of the graveyard, but under the watch of a foreign guard.

But the most important observation to be made about every concrete analysis of relations of forces is this: that such analyses cannot and must not be ends in themselves (unless one is writing a chapter of past history), and they only acquire significance if they serve to justify practical activity, an initiative of will. They show what are the points of least resistance where the force of will can be applied must fruitfully; they suggest immediate tactical operations; they indicate how a campaign of political agitation can best be presented, what language will be best understood by the multitudes, etc. The decisive element in every situation is the force, permanently organised and pre-ordered over a long period, which can be advanced when one judges that the situation is favourable (and it is favourable only to the extent to which such a force exists and is full of fighting ardour); therefore the essential task is that of paying systematic and patient attention to forming and developing this force, rendering it ever more homogeneous, compact, conscious of itself. One sees this in military history and in the care with which at all times armies have been predisposed to begin a war at any moment. The great States have been great precisely because they were at all times prepared to enter effectively into favourable international situations, and these situations were favourable because there was the concrete possibility of effectively entering them.

*Observations on some Aspects of the Structure of Political Parties in Periods of Organic Crisis*

At a certain point in their historical life social groups detach themselves from their traditional parties; i.e. the political parties, in that given organisational form, with the particular men who constitute, represent and lead them, are no longer recognised as the proper expression of their class or fraction of a class. When these crises occur, the immediate situation becomes delicate and dangerous, since the field is open to solutions of force, to the activity of obscure powers represented by "men of destiny" or "divine" men.

How are these situations of opposition between "represented and representatives" formed, situations which from the field of the parties (party organisations in the strict sense of the parliamentary-electoral field, newspaper organisation), are reflected throughout the whole State organism, strengthening the relative position of power of the bureaucracy (civil and military), of high finance, of the Church, and in general of all the organisms which are relatively independent of the fluctuations of public opinion? In every country the process is different, although the content is the same. And the content is a crisis of hegemony of the ruling class, which comes about either because the ruling class has failed in some big political undertaking for which it asked, or imposed by force, the consent of the broad masses (like war), or because vast masses (especially of peasants and petty-bourgeois intellectuals) have passed suddenly from political passivity to a certain activity and put forward aims which in their disorganic complex constitute a revolution. One speaks of a "crisis of authority" and this in fact is the crisis of hegemony, or crisis of the State in all spheres.

The crisis creates immediately dangerous situations, because the different strata of the population do not possess the same capacity for rapid reorientation or for reorganising themselves with the same rhythm. The traditional ruling class, which has a numerous trained personnel, changes men and programmes and reabsorbs the control which was escaping it with a greater speed than occurs in the subordinate classes; it makes sacrifices, exposes itself to an uncertain future by making demagogical promises, but it maintains power, strengthens it for the moment and makes use of it in order to crush its opponent and disperse its leading personnel, which cannot be very numerous or well-trained. The transference of the effectives of many parties under the banner of a single party which better represents and embodies the needs of the entire class, is an organic and normal phenomenon, even if its rhythm is very rapid and almost like a thunder-bolt in comparison with calm times: it represents the fusion of a whole social group under a single leadership which is alone considered capable of solving an existing, predominant problem and removing a mortal danger. When the crisis does not find this organic solution, but the solution of a divine leader, it means that there exists a static equilibrium (whose factors may be unequal, but in which the immaturity of the progressive forces is decisive); that no group, either conservative or progressive, has the force for victory and that even the conservative group needs a master.[1]

This order of phenomena is connected with one of the most im-portant questions relating to the political party; that is, to the capacity of the party for reacting against the spirit of habit, against the tendency to become mummified and anachronistic. Parties come into existence and are constituted organisationally in order to lead the situation in historically vital moments for their classes; but they are not always able to adapt themselves to new tasks and new periods, they are not always able to develop according to the development of the complex relations of force (and hence relative position of their classes) in the particular country or in the international field. In analysing this party development it is necessary to distinguish: the social group; the mass of the party; the bureaucracy and High Command of the party. The bureaucracy is the most dangerously habitual and conservative force; if it ends up by constituting a solid body, standing by itself and feeling independent from the masses, the party ends by becoming anachronistic, and in moments of acute crisis becomes emptied of all its social content, like an empty shell. One can see what happened to a number of German parties with the expansion of Hitlerism. The French parties are a rich field for this research they are all mummified and anachronistic, historico-political documents of different phases of past French history, whose outworn terminology they repeat; their crisis might become even more catastrophic than that of the German parties.

[1] cf. *The Eighteenth Brumaire of Louis Bonaparte.*

Those who examine this kind of event usually forget to give a correct place to the bureaucratic, civil and military, element, and in addition, do not keep in mind the fact, that such an analysis must not only include active military and bureaucratic elements, but also the social strata from which, in the given state complex, the bureaucracy is traditionally recruited. A political movement can be of a military character even if the army as such does not openly participate in it; a government can be of a military character even if the army as such does not openly participate in it. In certain situations it can happen that it is convenient not to "reveal" the army, not to make it step outside constitutionalism, not to bring politics among the soldiers, as it is said, in order to maintain homogeneity between officers and soldiers on a basis of apparent neutrality and superiority over factions; still it is the army, i.e. the General Staff and the officers, which determines the new situation and dominates it. On the other hand, it is not true that the army, according to the constitutions, must never be political; the army must in fact defend the constitution, i.e. the legal form of the State, together with its connected institutions; therefore the so-called neutrality means only support for the reactionary side; but it is necessary, in these situations, to pose the question in this way in order to prevent the army reproducing the dissent of the country which would lead to the disappearance of the determining power of the High Command through the disintegration of the military instrument. All these observations are certainly not absolute; at different historical moments and in various countries they have very different import.

## On Bureaucracy

(1) The fact that in the historical development of political and economic forms there has come to be formed a type of "career" functionary, technically trained for bureaucratic work (civil and military), has a primary significance in political science and in the history of State forms. Was it a matter of necessity or of a degeneration from self-government, as the "pure" liberals pretend? It is certain that every form of society and State has had its own problem of functionaries, its own way of presenting and solving it, its own system of selection, its own type of functionary to be educated. It is of capital importance to reconstruct the development of all these elements. The problem of

the functionaries partly coincides with the problem of the intellectuals. But, if it is true that every new form of society and State has had need of a new type of functionary, it is also true that new ruling social groups have never been able to put aside, at least for a certain time, the traditional and established interests, that is, the formation of functionaries already existing and preconstituted at the time of their advent (especially in the ecclesiastical and military sphere). Unity of manual and intellectual work and a closer link between the legislative and the executive power (by which the elected functionaries concern themselves with the execution of State affairs as well as with control), can be inspiring motives for a new line in the solution of the problem of the intellectuals as well as for that of the functionaries.

(2) Connected with the question of the bureaucracy and its "best" organisation is the discussion of so-called "organic centralism" and "democratic centralism" (which, on the other hand, has nothing to do with abstract democracy, since the French Revolution and the Third Republic have developed forms of organic centralism of which the absolute monarchy and Napoleon I knew nothing.) The real economic and political relationships which find their organisational form, their articulation and function in the different manifestations of organic and democratic centralism in all fields, will have to be researched into and examined: in State life (centralism, federation, union of federated States, federation of States or federal State, etc.); in inter-State life (alliances, various forms of international political "constellations"); in the life of political and cultural associations (Free Masonry, Rotary Club, Catholic Church); economic unions (cartels, trusts); in the same country, in different countries, etc.

Polemics arose in the past (before 1914) about the German predominance in the life of high culture and of some international political forces: was then this predominance real, or in what did it really consist? It can be said: (a) that no organic disciplinary link established this supremacy, which was therefore merely a phenomenon of abstract cultural influence and very shaky prestige; (b) that this cultural influence did not in any way concern effective activity, which vice versa was disconnected, local, without a unifying direction. One cannot speak therefore of any centralism, neither organic nor democratic nor of any kind or mixture. The influence was felt and sustained by small intellectual groups, without ties with the popular masses; and precisely this absence of ties characterised the situation. Nevertheless, such a state of affairs is worth examining because it is useful in explaining the process which led to the formulation of the theories of organic centralism, which were a one-sided criticism by intellectuals of disorder and dispersal of forces.

At the same time it is necessary to distinguish, in the theories of organic centralism, between those which conceal a precise programme of the real predominance of one party over everything (whether it is a party composed of a group, like that of the intellectuals or made up of a "privileged" territorial group) and those which are a purely one-sided standpoint of sectarians and fanatics, and which, though they may conceal a programme of predominance (usually of a single individual, like that of Papal infallibility by which Catholicism was transformed into a kind of cult of the Pope), do not immediately appear to conceal such a programme as a conscious political fact. The more correct name would be that of bureaucratic centralism. "Organicness" (*organicità*) can only come from democratic centralism which is "centralism" in movement, so to speak, that is, a continuous adjustment of the organisation to the real movement, a tempering of the thrusts from below with the command from above, a continuous intrusion of elements which emerge from the depths of the masses into the solid frame of the apparatus of rule, which assures continuity and the regular accumulations of experiences; it is "organic" because it takes account of the movement, which is the organic means for the revealing of historical reality and does not become mechanically stiffened in the bureaucracy, and, at the same time, it takes account of what is relatively stable and permanent or what at least moves in an easily foreseeable direction, etc. This element of stability in the State is embodied in the organic development of the central nucleus of the ruling group, just as happens on a more restricted scale in the life of parties. The prevalence of bureaucratic centralism in the State indicates that the ruling group is saturated, becoming a narrow clique which strives to perpetuate its selfish privileges by regulating or even suffocating the birth of opposing forces, even if these forces are homogeneous to the fundamental ruling interests (for example, in the protectionist systems in their struggle to the bitter end with economic liberalism). In parties which represent socially subordinate groups the element of stability is necessary in order to ensure hegemony not for privileged groups but for the progressive elements, organically progressive in comparison with other related and allied, but composite and wavering, forces.

In any case, it needs to be pointed out that unhealthy manifestations of bureaucratic centralism occurred because of a lack of initiative and responsibility below, that is, because of the primitive politics of the peripheral forces, even when these were homogeneous with the hegemonic territorial group (the phenomenon of Piedmontesism in the first decades of Italian unity). The formation of such situations can be extremely damaging and dangerous in international organisations (the League of Nations).

Democratic centralism provides an elastic formula, which lends itself to many embodiments; it lives to the extent to which it is continuously interpreted and adapted to necessity: it consists in the critical research into what is uniform in the apparent irregularity and on the other hand of what is distinctive and even contrasting in the apparent uniformity, in order to organise and connect closely together what is alike, but in such a way that the organising and connecting appears as an "inductive" and experimental necessity and not as the result of a rationalistic, deductive and abstractive process, that is, one which is peculiar to pure intellectuals (or pure asses). This continuous effort to separate the "international" and "unitary" element from the national and local reality is in fact concrete political action, the only activity which produces historical progress. It requires an organic unity between theory and practice, between intellectual groups and popular masses, between rulers and governed. From this point of view the formulæ of unity and federation lose a great part of their significance, while they preserve their poison in the bureaucratic conception, as a result of which we end up with no unity, but a stagnant marsh, superficially calm and "dumb", and with no federation, but a "sack of potatoes", i.e. a mechanical juxtaposition of individual "unities" without any link between them.

### The Theorem of Definite Proportions

This theorem can be usefully employed to make clearer certain arguments regarding the science of organisation (the study of the administrative apparatus, of demographic composition, etc.), giving them a plainer pattern, and also politics generally (in analyses of situations, relations of forces, in the problem of the intellectuals, etc.). It is understood that one always needs to remember how recourse to the theorem of definite proportions has a schematic and metaphorical value, that it cannot be applied mechanically, since in human aggregates the qualitative element (or the technical and intellectual ability of individual members) has a predominating function, whereas it cannot be measured mathematically. Therefore it can be said that every human aggregate has its own particular *best* principle of definite proportions.

The science of organisation especially can usefully refer to this theorem, and this can be seen clearly in the army. But every form of society has its own type of army and every type of army has its own principle of definite proportions, which also changes even for the different arms or specialities. There is a determined relationship between the troops, the non-commissioned officers, subalterns, superior officers, High Commands, the General Staff, etc. There is a relationship between the various arms and specialised bodies among them, etc. Any change in one part determines the need for a new balance for all, etc.

Politically the theorem can be seen applied in parties, trade unions, factories, and it can be seen how each social class has its own law of definite proportions, which varies according to the level of culture, of mental independence, spirit of initiative and sense of responsibility and of the discipline of its more backward and borderline members.

The law of definite proportions is summed up by Pantaleoni in this way in his *Principles of Pure Economics*: ". . . Bodies combine chemically only in definite proportions and each quantity of an element which exceeds the quantity required for combination with other elements, present in definite quantities, remains *free*; if the quantity of an element is too little in relation to the quantity of other elements present, combination only takes place to the extent to which there is sufficient quantity of the element which is present in *lesser quantity* than the others."

Use could be made metaphorically of this law in order to understand how a "movement" or a trend of opinion, becomes a party, that is, a political force which is effective from the point of view of the army of the governing power: precisely to the extent to which it possesses (has produced inside itself) leaders at various levels, and to the extent to which these leaders have acquired certain abilities. The historical "automatism" of certain premises (the existence of certain objective conditions) is potentialised politically by parties and by men of ability: their absence or weakness (quantitively and qualitatively) neutralises the "automatism" itself (which is therfore not automatism): the premises exist abstractly but the consequences are not realised because the human factor is lacking. Therefore parties can be said to have the task of elaborating capable leaders, they are the function of the masses which selects, develops, multiplies the necessary leaders in order that a definite social group (which is a "fixed" quantity, since it can be established how many members there are of each social group) articulates itself from confused chaos, becomes an organically predisposed political army. When a party in successive elections at the same level or at different levels (for example in pre-Hitler Germany: elections for the president of the republic, for the *Reichstag*, for the diets of the Länder, for the communal councils, and so on down to the factory committees), fluctuates in its mass of votes between a maximum and a minimum which appear strange and arbitrary, it can be deduced that its cadres are deficient in quantity and quality, or in quantity and not in quality (relatively), or in quality and not in quantity. A party which has many votes in local elections and less in those of greater political importance is certainly qualitatively deficient in its central leadership: it has many subordinates or at least a sufficient number, but it does not possess a High Command which is adequate for the country and for its position in the world, etc.

## Sociology and Political Science

The success of sociology is related to the decadence of the concept of political science and political art which appeared in the nineteenth century (more exactly in the second half, with the success of evolutionary and positivistic doctrines). What is really important in sociology is nothing but political science. "Politics" becomes synonymous with parliamentary politics or the politics of personal cliques. The conviction that with constitution and parliaments the epoch of "natural evolution" has begun, that society has found a definitive, because rational, basis, etc. So now society can be studied with the methods of the natural sciences. Impoverishment of the concept of State follows from this way of looking at things. If political science means science of the State and the State is the whole complex of practical and theoretical activities with which the ruling class not only justifies and maintains its rule but manages to win the active consent of the governed, it is obvious that all the essential questions of sociology are nothing but questions of political science. If there are some left over, these must be false problems, i.e. useless problems. The question presented to Bukharin was therefore one of determining in what relation political science could be placed with Marxism; if there is an identity between the two (which cannot be upheld, or can only be upheld from the point of view of shabby positivism), or if political science is the totality of empirical or practical principles which are deduced from a wider conception of the world or a philosophy in the true sense, or if this philosophy is only the science of concepts or general categories which arise from political science, etc.

If it is true that man can only be conceived of as historically determined, i.e. that he has developed and lived in certain conditions, in a determined social complex or totality of social relations, can sociology be conceived as only the study of these conditions and the laws which regulate their development? Since one cannot leave aside the will and and initiative of men themselves, this concept must be false. The problem should be posed of what is "science" itself. Is not science itself "political activity" and political thought, inasmuch as it transforms men, makes them different from what they were before? If everything is "politics" we must, in order not to fall into tautological and tiresome phraseology, distinguish with new concepts the politics which corresponds to that science which is traditionally called "philosophy" from the politics which is called political science in the strict sense. If science is the "discovery" of hitherto unknown reality, does not this reality come to be conceived as transcendent in a certain sense? Does one not think that something "unknown" and therefore transcendent still exists? And does not the concept of science as "creation" mean "politics"? It all rests on seeing whether we are talking about a creation which is "arbitrary" or rational, that is, useful to men in enlarging their views of life, in making life itself superior (develop).[1]

### Number and Quality in Representative Régimes

One of the more banal commonplaces which people go about repeating against the elective system of forming organs of State is this, that "number is the supreme law in this" and that "the opinions of any idiot who knows how to write (and even illiterates, in certain countries), are valid, in effectively determining the political course of the State, to exactly the same extent as those of the people who devote their best powers to the State and the nation, etc." But the fact is that it is not in any way true that number is the "supreme law", nor that the weight of the opinion of every elector is "exactly" the same. In this case also, numbers are simply an instrumental value, which offers a measure and a relationship and nothing more. What then is measured? What is measured is precisely the effectiveness and ability to expand and persuade of the opinions of a few people, of the active minorities, of the *élites*, of the advanced guards, etc., that is to say, their rationality, historicity or concrete functionalism. This means that it is not true that the weight of the opinions of single individuals is "exactly" the same. Ideas and opinions are not "born" spontaneously in the brains of each individual; they have had a centre of formation, of radiation, of propaganda, of persuasion, a group of men or even a single individual who has elaborated and presented them in their actual political form. The counting of "votes" is the concluding manifestation of a long process in which the greatest influence belongs precisely to those who "devote their best powers (such as they are) to the State and the nation". If this presumed group of patriarchs, despite the overwhelming material forces which it possesses, does not have the consent of the majority, it will have to be judged either inept or not representative of the "national" interests which are bound to be predominant in inducing the national will in one way rather than in another. "Unfortunately" everyone is led to confuse his own "particular" interests with those of the nation and therefore to find it "horrible", etc., that it is for the "law of numbers" to decide; surely it is better to become an *élite* by

[1] As regards the "Popular Study" and its appendix, *Theory and Practice*, the philosophical review of Armando Carlini, in *New Anthology* for March 16th, 1933, from which it emerges that the equation: "Theory : practice = pure mathematics : applied mathematics" has been promulgated by an Englishman (Whittaker, I think).

decree. The question therefore is not one of people who are intellectually "well off" and feel themselves reduced to the level of the last
illiterate, but of those who presume that they are well off and want to
take away from the "ordinary" man even that small fraction of power
which he possesses in deciding the course of State life.

From a criticism (originating in an oligarchy and not an *élite*) of
the parliamentary régime (it is strange that it has not been criticised
because the historical rationality of numerical consent has been syste-
matically falsified by the influence of wealth), these banal statements
have been extended to every representative system, even those which
are not parliamentary and not fashioned according to the canons of
formal democracy. These statements are all the more incorrect. In
these other régimes consent does not reach its final stage at the time of
voting, on the contrary.[1] Consent is supposed to be permanently
active, up to the point where the consentors could be considered as
"functionaries" of the State and the elections as a means of voluntary
enrolment of State functionaries of a certain type, which in a certain
sense could be linked (on different planes) with self-government. As
the elections take place not on general vague programmes but on programmes of immediate concrete work, those who consent pledge
themselves to do something more than the ordinary legal citizen in
order to realise them, that is, to be a vanguard of active and responsible
labour. The "voluntary" element in initiative could not be stimulated
in any other way for the largest multitudes, and when these are not
made up of amorphous citizens but of qualified productive elements,
one can understand the importance which the expression of the vote
can have.[2]

The proposition that "society does not set itself problems for whose
solution the material preconditions do not already exist". The problem
of the formation of a collective will depends directly on this proposition. To analyse critically what the proposition means, it is important
to research into how precisely permanent collective wills are formed,

[1] An allusion to the Soviet system of permanent control of the electors over the elected.
—*Trans.*

[2] These observations could be developed more fully and organically, pointing out the
other differences between the different types of electionism, according as the general
social and political relations change: relationship between elective and career functionaries, etc.

and how these wills set themselves direct and indirect concrete ends, that is, a line of collective action. We are dealing with more or less long processes of development, and rarely with unforeseen "synthetic" outbursts. Synthetic "outbursts" do occur, but looked at closely it is seen that they are more destructive than constructive, they remove external mechanical obstacles to an aboriginal and spontaneous development: the Sicilian Vespers can be taken as an example.

One could study concretely the formation of a collective historical movement, analysing it in all its molecular phases, which is usually not done because each treatment would become burdensome: instead, currents of opinion are assumed already constituted around a group or a dominating personality. It is the problem which in modern times is expressed in terms of a party or of a coalition of allied parties: how the constitution of the party begins, how its organised force and social influence develop, etc. We are dealing with a very detailed molecular process, one of extreme analysis, capillary, whose documentation consists of an overwhelming quantity of books, pamphlets, articles in reviews and journals, verbal conversations and debates which are repeated infinitely and which in their gigantic totality represent this long labour from which is born a collective will with a certain degree of homogeneity, that certain degree which is necessary and sufficient to determine an action co-ordinated and simultaneous in the time and geographical space in which the historical fact occurs.

The importance of utopias and of confused and rationalistic ideologies in the initial phase of the historical processes of formation of collective wills: utopias, abstract rationalism, have the same importance as the old conceptions of the world elaborated historically through the accumulation of successive experiences. What is important is the criticism to which this ideological complex comes to be subjected by the first representatives of the new historical phase: through this criticism we have a process of distinction and change in the relative influence which the elements of the old ideologies used to possess: what was secondary and subordinate or even incidental comes to be assumed as foremost, becomes the nucleus of a new ideological and doctrinal complex. The old collective will breaks up into its contradictory elements, because from these elements the subordinate ones develop socially, etc.

Since the formation of the party régime, an historical phase tied to the standardisation of large masses of the population (communications, newspapers, big cities, etc.), the molecular processes happen more rapidly than in the past, etc.

### Hegemony (Civil Society) and Division of Powers

The division of powers and the whole discussion which took place for its realisation, and the legal dogma which came into existence at its advent, are the result of the struggle between the civil society and the political society of a certain historical period, with a certain unstable balance of classes, determined by the fact that certain categories of intellectuals (in the direct service of the State, especially the civil and military bureaucracy) are still too much tied to the old ruling classes. That is, there occurs inside society what Croce calls the "perpetual conflict between Church and State", if the Church is taken to represent civil society in its totality (whereas it is only a proportionately less important element of it), and the State every attempt to cystallise permanently a determined stage of development, a determined situation. In this sense the Church itself can become State and the conflict can show itself between lay and laicising civil society and State-Church (when the Church has become an integral part of the State, of the political society monopolised by a certain privileged group which unites with the Church in order better to preserve its monopoly with the help of that zone of "civil society" represented by the Church).

The essential importance of the division of powers for political and economic liberalism: the whole liberal ideology, with its strengths and weaknesses, can be summed up in the principle of the division of powers, and the source of liberalism's weakness becomes apparent: it is the bureaucracy, i.e. the crystallisation of the leading personnel, which exercises coercive power and which at a certain point become a caste. Hence the popular aim of making all posts elective, an aim which is extreme liberalism and at the same time its dissolution (principle of the permanent Constitution, etc.; in republics the periodic election of the head of State gives an illusory satisfaction to this elementary popular aim).

Unity of the State in the distinction of powers: Parliament is more tied to civil society, the judiciary power is between government and

Parliament, represents the continuity of written law (against the government as well). Naturally all the three powers are also organs of political hegemony, but to a different extent: (1) Parliament; (2) magistracy; (3) government. It should be noted how miscarriages in the administration of justice create an especially disastrous impression among the public: the hegemonic apparatus is most sensitive in this sector, in which can also be included the arbitrary actions of the police and the political administration.

### The Conception of Law

A conception of law which must be essentially innovatory, cannot be found, integrally, in any already existing doctrine (not even in the doctrine of the so-called positivist school, and particularly in Ferri's doctrine). If every State aims to create and maintain a certain type of civilisation and citizen (and hence of life in common and individual relationships), it aims to make certain customs and attitudes disappear and to propagate others, law will be the instrument for this end (side by side with schools and other institutions and activities). It must be elaborated in order that it should conform to the end, and that it should have the maximum effect in producing positive results.

The conception of law will have to be freed from every remnant of transcendence and absoluteness; practically from all moralistic fanaticism; nevertheless it seems to me that it cannot begin from the point of view that the State does not "punish" (if this term is reduced to its human significance), but struggles only against social "danger-ousness". In reality the State must be seen as an "educator", in that it aims precisely to create a new type and level of civilisation. Because of the fact that it operates essentially on the economic forces, that it reorganises and develops the apparatus of economic production, that it alters the structure, one must not draw the conclusion that the events of the superstructure must be abandoned to themselves, to their spontaneous development, to a haphazard and sporadic germination. In this field as well the State is an instrument of "rationalisation", of acceleration and of Taylorisation, it works according to a plan, it presses, it arouses, it urges, and it "punishes", since, when the condi-tions are created in which a certain way of life is "impossible", "crim-inal action or omission" must have a punitive sanction, with a moral import, and not only a judgment of general dangerousness. Law is the repressive and negative aspect of the whole positive activity of civilising developed by the State. "Prize-giving" activities of individuals and groups should also be incorporated into the conception of law, etc.; praiseworthy and meritorious activity is rewarded just as criminal activity is punished (and it is punished in original ways, making "public opinion" play a part as a sanctioner).

## ERRATUM

TASCA. The biographical note on Angelo Tasca, page 192, is incorrect in stating that Tasca became director of the Communist Party newspaper *L'Unita* in 1945. Tasca was in fact expelled from the Communist Party of Italy in 1929.

# BIOGRAPHICAL NOTES AND GLOSSARY

BAKUNIN, Michael (1814-1876): Russian anarchist leader. Exiled to Siberia, Bakunin escaped to Italy in 1861 where he founded a secret international anarchist organisation known as the International Alliance of Social Democracy. In 1868 he joined the First International but separated from it in 1874 after disagreements both political and personal. Central to his ideas were a belief in complete freedom in all spheres and a belief in the natural solidarity of man.

BOULANGER: After the famous Wilson scandal in France in 1887, General Boulanger led a movement of Conservatives, Royalists and Radicals against the coalition government of the Republic. For a short period he enjoyed immense popularity. In 1889 he was elected for the Seine Department by a majority of 80,000 votes. The movement ended with his flight and suicide, in Brussels, in 1891. The main financial support for Boulanger came from the Monarchists.

BUKHARIN, Nikolai Ivanovich (1888-1938): Russian Communist leader and theoretician, was born in Moscow. He joined the Bolshevik faction of the Russian Social Democratic Party in 1906, and in 1912 he collaborated with Lenin in editing *Pravda*. After the Revolution Bukharin became a member of the Politburo. From 1926-1929 he played a prominent part in the Executive Committee of the Communist International. In 1934 he became editor of *Izvestia*, but in 1937 he was arrested on charges of conspiring with followers of Trotsky. In 1938 he was executed.

CAVOUR, Count Camillo Benso di (1810-1861): Italian statesman and architect of Italian unity. Having first been appointed Minister of Agriculture and Commerce in the Kingdom of Sardinia he rose rapidly to chief minister. It was his policy of economic and military development coupled with a shrewd international policy which helped to achieve what the national revolution of 1848-9 had failed to establish—Italian unity. But despite his temporary alliance with Garibaldi his methods were rather those of diplomacy than of revolution. The result of his work was the transformation of Piedmont into the Kingdom of Italy.

CROCE, Benedetto (1866-1954): Italian idealist philosopher, born at Pescasseroli in Apulia and educated at the University of Rome. In 1910 he became a senator and from 1920-1921 was Minister of Education in the Giolitti government. A strong opponent of fascism, Croce went into retirement during the Mussolini régime.

D'ANNUNZIO, Grabriele (1863-1938): Italian poet and adventurer. Supporter of fascism from its inception. Born at Pescara, D'Annunzio was educated at the Collegio Cicognini at Prato. He worked assiduously to induce Italy to enter the First World War. From 1915-1918 he served in the Army, and in 1919, with a small band of officers he seized Fiume in an attempt to prevent its going to Yugoslavia. D'Annunzio was greatly influenced by the ideas of Nietzsche.

DE LEON, Daniel (1852-1914): American Socialist leader, born in the Dutch West Indies. Lectured in International Law at Columbia University; then, after joining the Socialist Labour Party, he became in 1891 editor of the party's paper *The People*. In 1905 helped to form the *Industrial Workers of the World* (q.v.). Although a Marxist, he accepted many syndicalist ideas; but he favoured a centralised and militant labour movement and the participation of the workers in political struggle.

GENTILE, Giovanni (1875-1944): Italian philosopher and politician, appointed professor of the philosophy of history at Rome in 1918. In that year Gentile became a senator. He supported fascism from the start. Mussolini appointed him Minister of Education and from 1926 to 1928 he was president of the Supreme Council of Education. He was responsible for a revival of religious teaching in the schools. Assassinated at Florence on April 5, 1944.

GENTILONI PACT (1913): An important landmark in the history of relations between the Italian State and the Catholic Church. Count Gentiloni represented the interests of the Catholic electors in negotiating the pact with Giolitti, the Prime Minister. In return for the support of the Catholic deputies, Giolitti agreed not to mention divorce, not to tamper with the Church schools, and to respect other Catholic susceptibilities.

GIOLITTI, Giovanni (1842-1928): Italian statesman, was born at Mondori in Piedmont. In 1884 he was elected to the Chamber as a member of the Left, and in 1892 he became Premier. He was responsible for introducing fiscal reform and the kind of progressive legislation which in England was associated with Gladstone. He was inclined to be neutral or even sympathetic towards the growth of trade unions. In 1911 Giolitti introduced the law of universal suffrage. He showed some weakness towards fascism at first but in 1924 went over to the opposition.

INDUSTRIAL WORKERS OF THE WORLD (I.W.W.): A militant working class organisation, founded in the United States in 1905, whose aim was to unite all workers into one large union. It was not only aimed at bettering immediate conditions but also at the overthrow of the capitalist system. From 1905 to 1908 it was under socialist influence (v. DE LEON) but afterwards it came under syndicalist influence. It received support especially among the unskilled and immigrant workers who were throughly dissatisfied with the craft unionism and conservatism of the American Federation of Labour. The Industrial Unions, it was believed, could form the basis of the future socialist society, thus "forming the structure of the new society within the shell of the old". The I.W.W. played an important part in raising the class consciousness and fighting spirit of the unskilled workers of the U.S.A. After the First World War, however, the movement began to decline, as a result of very severe repression and internal dissension. Some I.W.W. leaders such as William Z. Foster later joined the American Communist Party.

LABRIOLA, Antonio (1843-1904): Italian Socialist philosopher, professor at the University of Rome, 1874-1904. A great teacher and controversialist, only a small portion of his ideas appear in his books. Influenced by Hegel, Herbart and Marx, he was an advocate of historical materialism.

LUXEMBURG, Rosa (1870-1919): One of the founders of the German Communist Party. Assassinated in 1919 by officers of the "Free Corps".

Author of *The Accumulation of Capital* (1913) and other important contributions to Marxist theory.

MICHELS, Robert: French sociologist, professor of political economy at Basle University and honorary professor at Turin University. Two of his books have been translated into English: *Political Parties: a sociological study of the oligarchical tendencies of modern democracy* (London, 1915), and *Eugenics in Party Organisation* (London, 1912).

POPULAR PARTY or *Partito Popolare*, a Catholic political party, in some senses the forerunner of the Christian Democratic Party of today. After the First World War the Vatican was at last reconciled to the formation of the Italian state and consequently it did not oppose the formation of the new party. It was founded in 1919 by a Sicilian priest, Don Luigi Sturzo. The basis of its programme was that though property itself was instituted by God, man can sometimes make a travesty of it. The party therefore defended the small property owners while attacking the landlord and capitalists. It had its right wing who regarded the party as a defence against socialism, and its left wing, those who were strongly influenced by the ideas of primitive Christianity. After 1919 it grew rapidly. That same year it had 101 deputies in Parliament; together with the Socialists, the "left" parties held half the seats in the Chamber. But they did not co-operate and made no attempt to form a government.

RED WEEK: This was the week in June 1914 when a general strike was called in Italy. The Red Flag was hoisted on the town hall of Bologna, and in the Romagna and the Marches a republic was declared. Order was more or less restored by the time of the outbreak of the World War in August, 1914.

SALVEMINI, Gaetano (b. 1873): Italian historian and publicist, was appointed to the chair of history at Florence in 1917. He edited the Liberal newspaper *L'Unità*. A vigorous critic of Giolitti's corrupt electoral methods and the half-heartedness of the socialists, Salvemini became an M.P. from 1919-1921. In 1925 he was arrested by the fascists but released provisionally soon afterwards; he left the country for the U.S.A. where he became a professor of history at Harvard University. Author of *Under the Axe of Fascism* (London, 1936).

SAVONAROLA, Fra Girolamo (1452-1498): Dominican friar who preached religious and civil reform in the Florentine Republic at the end of the 15th century. As preacher and prophet he inspired the revolution which in 1494 expelled the ruling house of Medici. But within four years his position had collapsed. In 1498 he was burnt as a heretic and false prophet. Machiavelli, who sympathised with many of his aims, despised his methods and termed him an 'unarmed prophet'.

SODERINI, Piero: Member of a leading Florentine family at the end of the 15th century he sided with the popular faction in the short-lived republic of 1494-1512. In 1502 he was elected chief magistrate of the Republic for life in an attempt to bring stability into the constantly shifting political life of the city. In this office he worked closely with Machiavelli who was secretary of the Republic. When the Republic was overthrown by force in 1512 both Machiavelli and Soderini were exiled.

SONNINO, Sidney, Baron (1847-1922): Italian statesman and financier, born in Florence. Noted for an exhaustive study of the conditions of the

Sicilian and Tuscan peasants. In 1877 he published, in co-operation with Leopoldo Franchetti, his work on Sicily (*La Sicilia*). Elected Deputy in 1880 and in 1893 became Minister of Finance during a severe monetary crisis. Prime Minister 1906-1909; Foreign Minister 1914-1919.

SOREL, Georges (1847-1922): French philosopher, theoretician of revolutionary syndicalism (q.v.). He was a pessimist with a strong conviction of the moral degeneration of the bourgeoisie. He attacked the idea of inevitable human progress. In his book, *Réflexions sur la Violence*, Sorel attempted a synthesis of Marxist ideas of class struggle with the ideas of Proudhon. Sorel combatted any idea that social change was historically and economically determined; the victory of the working class depended on its own militancy, and in this the "myth of the general strike" would play an important part. He was less interested in the workers fighting for higher wages than in creating a social élite of "heroes" who would usher in a new civilisation as a result of a "social war". (*See* SYNDICALISM.)

SYNDICALISM: Derived from the French word *syndicat*, a local trade union. Syndicalism is an offshoot of the ideas of anarchist-communism. Sorel and Pelloutier are looked on as its chief exponents. They placed special emphasis on the use of the trade unions in creating a new society. The unions in a certain locality should jointly operate all industries in that area; then these self-governing communities should form themselves into a loose federation. The syndicalists were opposed to the state and centralisation in any form; they urged the workers to ignore political parties. They relied on short strikes to better their conditions, but were against building up union funds or coming to agreements with employers as this would reduce the militancy of the workers. They put forward the aim of the "general strike to overthrow capitalism", but Sorel regarded this as only a "necessary myth". Syndicalism was strongest in France and Spain—especially Catalonia where it still exerts influence.

TASCA, Angelo: Italian communist leader, born at Moretta in 1892. A syndicalist of Turin he worked closely with Gramsci, Togliatti and Terracini. After the Livorno Congress, 1921, Tasca joined the Italian Communist Party. During the fascist period he lived in France, Germany and Russia, returning to Italy in 1945 to become director of the Party's newspaper *L'Unità*.

TURATI, Filippo (1857-1932): Italian socialist leader, was born into a well-to-do Lombardy family. In 1890 he became editor of *Critica Sociale* the organ of the socialist intelligentsia, and in 1896 he was elected to Parliament. Turati was a leader of the reformist section of the socialists. He urged them to abandon revolutionary methods and realise their aims through gradual reforms and constitutional methods. However, all the institutions he had helped to create, such as trade unions, co-operatives and educational bodies, were destroyed one by one by the fascist government after 1922. Turati himself escaped to Corsica in 1926 and died in Paris.

VICO, Giambattista (1668-1744): Neapolitan philosopher. His great work is his *Scienza Nuova*. Vico believed that history could provide knowledge no less certain than natural science. Vico put forward the idea that history was the process of the rise and fall of civilisations; each civilisation, he thought, goes through the age of gods, the age of heroes and the age of man, after which it declines into barbarism when the whole cycle begins again.